BALANCED READING INSTRUCTION

Teachers' Visions and Voices

Edited by
Jerry L. Johns
Laurie Elish-Piper
Northern Illinois University

KENDALL/HUNT PUBLISHING COMPANY
4050 Westmark Drive   Dubuque, Iowa 52002

Editors' Address:
Jerry L. Johns/Laurie Elish-Piper
Northern Illinois University
Reading Clinic—119 Graham Hall
DeKalb, IL 60115

Cover photograph: Images © 1996 PhotoDisc, Inc.
Text photographs: Susan Johns and Gary Meader, Sumas, WA

Printed in the United States of America
10   9   8   7   6   5   4   3   2   1

Contents

Acknowledgments

Teachers played a vital role in every aspect of this project. Their experiences, ideas, and insights guided the process of developing this book from start to finish. Specifically, we would like to thank Linda Hursh, Mary Keil, Dave Meyer, and Teri Schuster, teachers who were instrumental in helping us select manuscripts for this book. These same individuals, along with Barbara Abromitis, Deborah Augsburger, Dorie Cannon, Donna Haney, Beth Johns, and Laura Porter, read near-final versions of the articles and provided useful feedback and helpful suggestions. We appreciate their attention to both big ideas and details.

Barb Meredith has been a wonderful secretary for over six years. The cheerful manner in which she made revision after revision is appreciated greatly. She has been a valuable partner in bringing the book to completion. Jamie Zaboroski and Anna Schaber, student workers in the Northern Illinois University Reading Clinic, have helped with proofing and other aspects of finalizing the manuscript. We appreciate their fresh look at and careful attention to fulfilling various tasks.

Books are the result of the talents shared by many people. We are grateful to all of you.

Jerry and Laurie

Editors

Jerry L. Johns is a Distinguished Teaching Professor and Director of the Reading Clinic at Northern Illinois University. Previously, he taught grades K-8 in the public schools and served as a reading teacher. He has also been a Visiting Professor at Western Washington University and the University of Victoria.

In addition to his major teaching responsibilities, Dr. Johns has been president of the Northern Illinois Reading Council, the Illinois Reading Council, and the College Reading Association. In addition, Dr. Johns has served on the Board of Directors of the International Reading Association. His more than 400 presentations and workshops for professional organizations and school systems have involved travel to Canada, the South Pacific, England, South America, and a majority of the United States.

Dr. Johns has authored numerous publications, including his well known *Basic Reading Inventory*—now in its seventh edition—and the second edition of *Improving Reading: A Handbook of Strategies*. He has also authored nearly 300 articles, monographs, pamphlets, and research studies. He was the associate editor of a national journal now called *Reading Research and Instruction*. Dr. Johns has also served on several editorial advisory boards for professional journals (e.g., *Reading Psychology*, *Reading & Writing Quarterly*). This is his tenth book.

Dr. Johns has been the recipient of numerous awards for his contributions to local, state, and national reading organizations. He received the Outstanding Service Award from the College Reading Association and was honored by the Illinois Reading Council with induction into the Reading Hall of Fame. Other recognitions include honorary membership in the Golden Key National Honor Society and the Alpha Delta Literacy Award (a local IRA honor society) for Scholarship, Leadership, and Service to Adult Learners. His most recent honor is the A.B. Herr Award for outstanding contributions to the field of reading.

Laurie Elish-Piper is an assistant professor of reading in the Department of Curriculum and Instruction at Northern Illinois University. She has taught grades 5–8 in public and private schools and served as an educational therapist for children ages 8–12 in an acute care psychiatric hospital.

Dr. Elish-Piper currently teaches undergraduate and graduate reading courses and supervises graduate students in practicum courses. She is also involved in several university-school partnerships which allow her to work closely with public school teachers, preservice teachers, and elementary students.

Dr. Elish-Piper is active in presenting research findings and classroom teaching strategies at national, state, and local conferences. Her research, presentations, and writing focus on family literacy, teaching diverse students, and authentic assessment. Her articles have appeared in the *Journal of Adolescent and Adult Literacy*, *The College Reading Association Yearbook*, *Illinois Reading Council Journal*, *Exploring Adult Literacy*, and *The Writing Teacher*. She has also written a chapter entitled, "Strengthening Reading Through Writing" for the second edition of *Improving Reading: A Handbook of Strategies*.

Dr. Elish-Piper is very involved in professional organizations, and she is currently the chair of the Adult Learning Division of the College Reading Association. Dr. Elish-Piper is a member and faculty advisor of Alpha Delta (a local IRA honor society). She is also on the editorial board of the College Reading Association's electronic Journal, *Exploring Adult Literacy*. This is her first book.

Contributors

Bryn Biesiadecki is a second year teacher. She is teaching first grade in the 1996–1997 school year. Bryn enjoys reading, movies, and spending time with her friends and family.

Janene Bowden is currently a substitute teacher, grades K-12. She has taught first grade and sold real estate. Janene enjoys her family, vacations, movies, house building, and remodeling.

Melisa Bower is a first-grade teacher at Kaneland School District #302 in Maple Park, Illinois. She has taught first grade for eight of her nine years in teaching. One year was spent at the fourth-grade level. Melisa enjoys reading, music, gardening, and spending time with her family.

Linda Conrad is an educator in the Kaneland School District #302. She has taught intermediate grades for twenty years. Linda enjoys teaching, traveling, flower gardening, photography, history, and computers. She is also a church organist and a "summer" insurance agent.

Beth Cowman is a second-grade teacher in Winnebago, Illinois. She has taught for almost 20 years. For ten of those years she was a substitute teacher in kindergarten through grade twelve. For the last nine years, she has been in her present position. Beth enjoys flower gardening, riding horses, reading mystery novels, traveling, and watching her children play various sports.

Jenelle Gallagher-Mance has been teaching the primary grades for six years in the suburbs of Chicago. Her experiences include first grade, second grade, and first/second grade multi-age teaching. While raising her two-year-old son, Jenelle enjoys gardening, biking, collecting baskets, and training her labrador retriever with her husband. She currently teaches first grade at Highlands Elementary School in LaGrange, Illinois.

Dawn Hinz is a fourth year teacher. She has taught first through third grade. Dawn enjoys aerobics, reading, and gardening.

Mary Kelly is a middle school reading specialist. She has been a reading specialist or language arts teacher in grades two through eight. She has also taught English as a second language, adult basic education, and has taught in workplace literacy programs.

Ann Kimpton is a reading and English teacher at Willowbrook High School in Villa Park, Illinois. She has a M.S.Ed. in Reading from Northern Illinois University and a B.A. in English Education from the University of Illinois. She and her husband live a balanced suburban life with their two children.

Jocelyn Klotz is a second-grade teacher in St. Charles, Illinois, and a graduate student in reading at Northern Illinois University. This is her fourth year of teaching. She was a member of her district's Standards and Assessment Committee for two years. Jocelyn enjoys spending time with her family and friends, gardening, aerobics, reading, and watching movies.

Suzie Lobdell teaches first grade at Ardmore Elementary School in Villa Park, Illinois. She has also taught inner-city children of Hispanic descent. She enjoys tennis, traveling, playing video games, and going to the movies.

Linda Mast is currently teaching first grade in Elk Grove Village, Illinois, and has completed a master's degree in reading. She has taught students in both first and second grades. Linda lives with her husband in Carol Stream and enjoys reading, movies, bike riding, and spending time with family and friends.

Jeanne McCarthy has been a Title I reading teacher at Kaneland Elementary School in Maple Park, Illinois, for the past eighteen years. She is the mother of three grown children and has one granddaughter. She lives in DeKalb, Illinois, with her husband, an art professor at Northern Illinois University.

Dorothy S. Strickland is the State of New Jersey Professor of Reading at Rutgers University, New Brunswick, New Jersey. She is a past president of the International Reading Association.

Loria Thatcher is a third-grade teacher at Madison Elementary School in Hinsdale, Illinois (District #181). She has taught third grade for three years. Last year, when she taught in Plainfield, Illinois, she was a recipient of the 1996 Board of Education Award of Teaching Excellence. Loria enjoys reading John Grisham books, watching movies, and exercising.

Christine Truckenmiller is a second-grade teacher at Immanuel Lutheran School in Freeport, Illinois. She is currently pursuing graduate studies at Northern Illinois University in DeKalb. She enjoys reading, movies, and camping.

Cynthia Vandergriff is a teacher at Palos East School in Palos Heights, Illinois. She has taught first grade for five years and second grade for one year. Cynthia teaches in a multi-year grouping situation—she takes her first grade class with her to second grade. She received her master's degree in reading from Northern Illinois University. Cynthia enjoys reading mysteries, watching movies, and exercising.

Rhonda L. Waggoner is a first-grade teacher at Dorthy Simon Elementary School in Winnebago, Illinois. She has taught for seven years: two years as a Title I Reading Teacher and five years as a first-grade teacher. She enjoys camping, hiking, and playing volleyball.

Introduction

A call for balanced reading programs is being heard within and beyond the borders of the United States. Several events have influenced a call for balance in reading instruction. Rightly or wrongly, test scores appear to have contributed to the call for balance. In California, for example, declining reading scores on the National Assessment of Educational Progress and state reports were considered by a Reading Task Force representing teachers, parents, principals, business people, superintendents, community members, professors, and school board members. One of the recommendations of the task force focused on a balanced reading program that would combine skill development with literature and language-rich activities (The Report of the California Reading Task Force, 1995).

Explicit, systematic skills instruction was prominent in the recommendation. In various states, this call for skills became political in the sense that bills were introduced into various state legislatures (e.g., North Carolina, Ohio, Texas, and Wisconsin) requiring specific teacher education coursework in reading. Such coursework often had a singular focus—phonics. The result, whether or not the bills ultimately passed, was a resurgence of phonics and its role in the teaching of reading.

As the phonics debate took shape and spread among large segments of society, certain methods came under close scrutiny: whole language and literature-based instruction. Some claimed that there were holes in whole language because skills (such as phonics) were not being taught. Others noted that students read quality literature but did not receive quality instruction in needed skills. Claims and counterclaims often pitted one group against another while teachers were busy engaging their students in a wide variety of literacy activities.

The quest for balanced reading programs will likely continue in the 21st century. Teachers who have contributed articles to this book represent a view from the classroom regarding balanced reading instruction in the early stages of what is likely to become a widespread movement. As you read this book, you will be presented with many voices and varied visions. Some of these teachers are veterans; others have recently joined the profession. You will feel the frustration of some teachers involved in a changing curriculum with nonexistent or limited staff development programs who, nevertheless, strive to provide quality reading instruction to average, struggling, and advanced readers. You will also read about other teachers who describe their successes and personal commitment to balanced reading instruction.

You will gain knowledge about the important aspects of what these teachers believe comprise a balanced program. And you will be challenged with issues to ponder as you consider balance in your reading program. We believe that the articles will stimulate educators to reduce, or perhaps boldly eliminate, one-way thinking about methods, skills, grouping, and assessment. We invite you to join the teachers in this volume in the search for those critical elements that will lead to reading programs where students learn to read and choose to read throughout their lives.

Jerry and Laurie

Setting the Stage

The word balance means harmonious or in proper arrangement when all aspects are considered. In a balanced reading program, the delicate balance among the various components, teacher roles, and teaching methodologies must be determined by the individual teacher based on the characteristics of his or her students, school, and community. While we feel there is no one answer to the question, "What's a balanced reading program?," Dorothy Strickland provides a useful overview of some of the issues that are likely to surface in the quest for balance. As you read her ideas, think about how they relate to your own teaching experiences and consider how the teachers' voices in this book might address and expand upon her insights.

In Search of Balance: Restructuring Our Literacy Programs

Dorothy S. Strickland

New insights into learning and teaching have brought numerous changes in literacy instruction. Greater emphasis on writing and its relationship to reading, greater use of trade books, and increased attention to the integration of the language arts are among the most noticeable changes. Most agree there is much to celebrate. Some would add that a measure of confusion and frustration often accompanies the changes.

A variety of factors may account for this. At times, new ideas are embraced and implementation attempted before the ideas are clearly understood. At other times, change is only nominally accepted by some individuals, leading them to impose old, familiar methods on new curricular frameworks.

In some cases, too many changes are imposed at once. Teachers complain about feeling overwhelmed as they attempt to implement several curricular innovations simultaneously.

Often teachers unwittingly misrepresent change. Comments such as "They don't let us teach phonics any more!" might actually reflect a policy that replaces a reliance on phonics workbooks with more effective approaches to teaching word recognition strategies—a change difficult for some teachers to accept.

Still another key problem resides in the inability of some of the leading proponents of change to make their case with the public or with large numbers of educators who see neither the need nor the advantages of the changes proposed. Despite all these factors, sweeping reforms have occurred, and educators are now faced with varying degrees of resistance against them.

From *Reading Today* (1996, October/November), 32. Reprinted with the permission of Dorothy S. Strickland.

The Search for Balance

Today, in districts throughout the United States, educators are once again reexamining the direction they have taken. They are wondering: "Have we gone too far in one direction or another? Have we abandoned some of the tried and true good practices of the past?" They want to know how they can take advantage of the best research and practice available in a way that makes sense and is most effective for students, teachers, and parents. They are searching for balance, a pursuit in which certain issues inevitably surface.

Here are some of the issues and my suggestions for how they might be addressed:

Balancing a Skills Emphasis With a Meaning Emphasis

Neither skills nor meaning need ever be abandoned. Skills are worthless as isolated knowledge, but they are powerful as strategies used purposefully and skillfully. Skills are learned best when taught through meaningful use.

For example, after sharing a story that includes many examples of the same sound/letter correspondence, highlight that relationship by pointing it out and discussing it with students. It might be the sound/letter relationship for the letter "b" or the inflectional ending "ing." Help children generalize to other instances by noting or collecting more examples. Encourage them to apply, in their spelling and writing, what they have learned about language through their reading and vice versa.

Balancing Direct and Indirect Instruction

Direct instruction usually refers to the explicit transmission of knowledge. Indirect instruction involves providing opportunities for children to apply skills that have been taught, to discover new ideas and strategies, and to assist one another as teachers and learners. Effective teaching will make use of both.

For example, minilessons are key elements of contemporary literacy instruction. These are systematically planned, brief instructional episodes that focus on a single strategy for learning and employ direct instructional teaching methods. Minilessons make heavy use of modeling and demonstration of skills in use. Teachers not only tell; they show. Showing someone how something is done may be the best type of direct instruction available.

Still, that is not enough. For students to "own" a skill and be able to use it strategically, they need opportunities to try it out on their own and to "discover" opportunities for its use. Adept teachers plan for a variety of opportunities for students to learn and apply what they know in meaningful ways.

Balancing Content and Process

Learning is much more than accumulating information. Yet getting information is frequently what inspires us to learn. Nevertheless, if we overemphasize content at the expense of process, children are left not knowing how to get information or to learn on their own.

For example, when teachers plan for instruction in science or social studies, they need to keep both content and process goals in mind. Content goals refer to the knowledge we hope students will gain from the topic under study. Specifically, this might refer to how plants grow or the roles of local government officials.

Process goals refer to what we hope students will learn to do as a result of their study. For example, they might learn how to interview a school board member or legislator and write a brief paragraph to share with the class. Or they might learn how to observe and chart the growth of seedlings over a period of time. Process goals take students beyond specific subject matter and help them to be skillful learners no matter what content is under study.

Balancing Trade Books and Textbooks

In many school districts, textbooks continue to act as core materials in various curricular areas. They provide a sense of continuity across grade levels. Nevertheless, students need to work with a wide variety of materials including authentic, quality literature. An effective literacy program will include an abundance of trade books.

It may be helpful to think of several layers of texts in the classroom. One layer might involve the literature selected by the teacher for read-aloud purposes. Another might be the textbooks in the core literacy program, involving all children in large and small groups and extending the information and ideas gained to trade books and technology. Yet another layer would include a variety of self-selected materials, which children would read and respond to independently as individuals or in small groups.

While these layers refer specifically to the literacy program, children should be involved with both core and trade book materials in every subject area. Each layer has an important role to play in a balanced program of instruction.

Balancing Informal Classroom Assessment and Norm-Referenced Standardized Tests

Shifting the balance away from standardized tests toward authentic classroom assessment is a goal that more educators applaud. High-stakes standardized tests are useful in rank-ordering pupils, schools, and school districts. However, they do little to help teachers focus on instructional needs. Consequently, educators are seeking to make greater use of performance-based assessment procedures, which are closely linked to the curriculum.

For example, portfolios that include samples of a student's writing over time help both teacher and student monitor specific strengths and weaknesses. On-going assessment of this type makes instructional criteria explicit for students, teachers, and others who need or wish to know.

A Word of Caution

This discussion of achieving balance in our literacy programs is not meant to imply that there is one specific Balanced Approach. Nor should it suggest a sampling method in which a little of this and a little of that are mixed together to form a grouping of disparate approaches euphemistically termed "eclectic." Finally, balance does not mean having two very distinct, parallel approaches coexisting in a single classroom in the name of "playing it safe"—for example, literature-based instruction on Mondays and Wednesdays and skills worksheets the remainder of the week.

Ultimately, one must make instructional decisions based on how children learn and how they can best be taught. More than likely this will never mean throwing out all of the methods used by any single teacher or school district. Nor will it mean maintaining the status quo. It will require an informed philosophical stance upon which to base instructional decisions.

Reform is never easy. In a climate where schools are constantly asked to do more with less and where school bashing gets votes and sells to the media, it may hardly seem worth the effort. Yet we have come too far to go backwards. Keep in mind that the changes currently under reconsideration were a response to dissatisfaction with what some recall as the "good" old days.

I know about the good old days. I was there. My recollection of those days makes me rejoice in the increased reading of real literature and the amount of writing that I see in many schools throughout the United States. In these schools, students know far more about books and authors than the students I recall in the past. Moreover, they have a sense of their own ability to generate questions and investigate the answers using their own knowledge and language power.

Achieving informed balance takes knowledge, time, and thoughtfulness. But it is well worth the effort.

Panoramic Views

The articles in this section represent a broad over-view of balanced reading instruction. The lead article offers a perspective from a teacher with nearly twenty years of experience. Her descriptions of professional struggles and growth provide valuable insights for edu-cators at all stages of their careers. The journey contin-ues with articles by two teachers who have much less experience. These teachers highlight some of the goals, reasons, and areas that characterize a balanced reading program. All three teachers offer insight into some of their professional and personal challenges as they strive to achieve a balanced reading program.

Attempting Takeoff: The Metamorphosis of a Reading Teacher

Jeanne McCarthy

As a teacher, I often felt like the caterpillar in Eric Carle's book, *The Very Hungry Caterpillar* (1969). Like that caterpillar, I experienced a metamorphosis. In the beginning of my journey, I gobbled up bits and pieces of information about reading instruction, much like the caterpillar who ate everything in sight without much discrimination. I hoped that, like the caterpillar, my metamorphosis would lead me to eventually "take off"—not to fly like the butterfly in Carle's story, but to confidently create balance in my teaching.

The "takeoff" was postponed many times over the years as a result of the many changes and trends in the field of reading instruction. Just as I was feeling comfortable with one approach, another would surface and I would lose my equilibrium. Without balance, it is difficult to fly and impossible to design an effective reading program.

As a classroom teacher in the early 1960's, I taught reading in the traditional basal manner. Even as a neophyte, I found teaching with the basal tedious. I was an avid reader as a child and had many memories of wonderful books. The basal stories I used lacked the excitement and imagination of real children's books.

It was at this time that I began my quiet revolt against using a pure basal approach. I secretly skipped some stories that I dreaded teaching and "forgot" to teach some low utility phonics skills. My right-brain thinking style made it so difficult to deal with the stilted comprehension questions in the teaching manual that I created my own. My instincts guided these decisions and I trusted them.

The language textbook was also a problem. Fill-in-the-blank type lessons were drudgery for my students and for me. After a while, I packed the books away and encouraged my class to write their own stories and reports. Examples of their writing were projected on an overhead and the class and I discussed ways to improve their writing. This certainly wasn't process writing, but it was an improvement and quite progressive for the early 1960's.

I left teaching for awhile to raise my family, but I returned to the halls of academe in the middle 1970's. While working on a graduate degree in reading, I was introduced to the language experience approach, informal reading inventories, and many ideas and trends that had surfaced during my hiatus.

In 1978, I was hired as a Title I Reading Teacher and began to see some inklings of real change on the horizon. Because of the progressive articles I had read about using real literature in reading programs, trade books were now a part of my Title I curriculum. Due to administrative constraints, this was a luxury not afforded to many classroom teachers, but because I was a reading specialist working in a Title I Program, I was able to develop a collection of trade books. Realizing that it was important for my students to do more actual reading, I eliminated some drill work and worksheets. I kept most of what was going on in my classroom undercover because, once again, my thinking about reading instruction was not in tune with the times.

About this same time, more articles began to appear in professional journals with titles such as, "Confessions of a Literature Lover" and "I Teach Reading With Real Books." The unconventional wisdom about literature-based programs made sense to me and confirmed my own beliefs about reading instruction. As a result, I took a risk and presented a workshop for my elementary principal and the teaching staff at my school. I shared the progressive journal articles and some of my own ideas about teaching reading, and encouraged my colleagues to use trade books in their own classrooms. I suggested that children learn to read by reading and recommended that teachers use fewer worksheets with their students and spend more time on the task of actually reading. Little did we know at the time that we were on the cutting edge of the whole language movement. Most teachers I have encountered have a solid knowledge base and good instincts, but lack the professional confidence to act on them. I believe my workshop gave some staff members the incentive to reevaluate their reading programs and make some positive changes.

Teaching reading is a "risky business" and like most things in life, you sometimes have to go "out on a limb" like a caterpillar and risk change in order to grow. Unfortunately, some teachers lack not only courage but adequate background information to implement these changes. Perhaps more in-service programs are necessary in order to support teachers during transitional times. John Manning suggests, "Part of the reason we find ourselves continually in a reading curriculum muddle is that we encourage very few long-duration, evolving, truly objective staff development programs" (Manning, 1995, p. 655). Monitoring by experienced and knowledgeable members of the school's staff would also be useful when introducing new ideas into the curriculum.

Shortly after I "came out of the closet" both literally (I moved to a larger classroom) and figuratively, the whole language movement took off with full force. It was a liberating experience and somewhat satisfying for me to have already had some experiences with whole language activities. With all the wonderful support from the expert opinions of reading authorities, I embraced whole language with enthusiasm. This excitement was short lived, however, because after a time, I realized that my Chapter 1 students were not progressing as they had done in the past. At this stage of my metamorphosis, I had some real doubts about the instructional direction I should take, and at one point, I wondered if I would ever "take off."

About this time I could have used some lessons in flying from Carle's butterfly. Maybe butterflies just emerge and take off, but struggling readers do not. To learn to fly, you need many skills, and learning to read is no different. Simply immersing children in literature does not guarantee that they will emerge as readers. More often than not, they don't.

During this time, the debate between whole language advocates and those who favored the traditional basal approach with structured phonics instruction was in full force. Diegmueller (1996a) described the debate: "The leading proponents of these distinct approaches have been lobbing bombs at one another in education journals and at conferences. Their passionate efforts to undermine each other have become known in education circles as 'the great reading war.'" This article further states that, "mounting empirical research indicates that many children need explicit phonics instruction, leading experts to suggest that a combination of the two approaches may be the most effective way to teach the beginning readers" (Diegmueller, 1996a, p. 20).

The liberation caused by the whole language movement was especially exciting for a right-brained, creative teacher, but I knew I had to return to reality, reevaluate what I was doing, and return to a more structured curriculum. This realization meant more time on the difficult task of teaching struggling readers and less time on creative activities. Art projects such as creating life-sized red Cliffords and producing imaginative plays and puppet shows are wonderful fun and have their place, but in my experience, struggling readers need a program that deals with actual reading activities.

Over the years, I have attended many wonderful workshops that tempted me to use exciting, creative activities in my classrooms. My imaginative right brain and the practical left side have struggled many times over how to balance the affective domain and the pragmatic in my reading program. I have come to believe that a practical approach for struggling readers seems to be the best answer. I don't mean to imply that the entire program is without any imaginative activities, but for the most part, the emphasis is on reading instruction. I appease my artistic nature by choosing enjoyable books that stimulate my students' imaginations and instill in them a love of reading.

I was pleased to read, some years later, John Manning's thoughts on this same issue.

> *Given the task of choosing activities related to the care of classroom pets, seasonal art, or other chronic aesthetic efforts, simulated historical events, plays and other "creative" pupil endeavors, or the onerous but essential task of pupil confrontation with written text, the choice of teachers and pupils is often all too obvious. And if it were, which is most often not the case at all, but if it were that these classroom accoutrements were a means to an end of a reading activity and toward an increase of reading fluency, the time spent and the student distraction tolerated could be justified. Quite frankly, many school administrators allow and many classroom teachers promote admittedly pacifying pleasurable classroom activities that avoid the most arduous task of teaching children to read in school.*

> *Every reasonable effort must be made to increase the amount of time spent teaching children to read in school, encouraging them to practice their learned skills, and motivating them to the highest levels of literary reflection (Manning, 1995, p. 653).*

Manning's message is that teachers, especially teachers of struggling readers, need to spend more time on the task of teaching reading and helping students reflect on what they have read. Reflecting on what has been read is essential. Brian Cambourne explains this in one of his principles of engagement: "Discussion and reflection are language processes that are fundamental to human learning. Both have a similar purpose in learning, namely, to explore, transact and clarify meaning" (Cambourne, 1995, p. 188).

As I reflect on the past, it appears that I have almost come full circle in my career as a reading teacher. I have truly been doing a balancing act all these years and hopefully I have come through all of these changes with some perspective and direction for the present and future.

I have some real concerns about the way today's schools are dealing with struggling readers. As a result of the whole language movement and whole class instruction, I believe that many of these students both in my school and throughout the country are being neglected in many classrooms.

One of the most basic considerations in the teaching of reading is that students should be instructed in books at their own level. This is not happening in some classrooms where there is whole class instruction. Regie Routman (1996) discusses this issue:

> *In selecting books to use in teaching reading, we need to consider text difficulty and students' interest and experiences. When a child makes many miscues (unexpected responses during oral reading), it usually means that the book or text is too hard and that the child should be given an easier selection. Developing readers make no progress in reading when they are continually given texts that are too difficult. In fact, they may regress. Yet, in many classrooms, children are regularly given books that are too challenging for them (Routman, 1996, p. 83).*

I know for a fact that in my own school there are many teachers instructing students as a class and using a grade level reading text. Struggling readers are very frustrated and Title I teachers (our name has come full circle) are left to pick up the pieces. Rather than supporting a child's classroom instruction, some Title I teachers are now providing the struggling student's entire reading program. Teaching struggling readers is difficult enough with the classroom teacher's support, but without this help, it is almost impossible.

I have come to the conclusion, as I reflect on my personal experiences in the field of reading, that a little common sense goes a long way in making decisions about creating a balanced reading program. To keep this balance in your teaching is a difficult task, and to accomplish it, you must have some conviction about what you believe works and what doesn't. Like the metamorphosis of a butterfly, the refinement and growth of a reading teacher takes time, but eventually it is possible to "take off" with confidence.

Dodging the Educational Pendulum: A Journey Toward A Balanced Language Curriculum

Melisa J. Bower

My teaching journey began in 1987 with my first full-time position after receiving my undergraduate degree in 1983. I have made changes in methodology, materials, and organization over the nine years of my career as the educational pendulum and administrative mandates have swung. In this article, I will explore my evolution with regard to language instruction, ranging from a skills-oriented curriculum to an attempt at a whole language philosophy, and the current search for a proper balance of strategies to ensure quality teaching.

Whole Language

In the summer of 1989 I attended a whole language workshop sponsored by the Northern Illinois Reading Council, where I had the privilege of seeing Bob and Marlene McCracken present their philosophies and ideas. The McCrackens suggested that children must work with language that is purposeful and meaningful before understanding can take place. Thus, one must first work with the whole and then the parts. Though this was obvious to some, for me it was a whole new view of language instruction.

Armed with new enthusiasm and wonderful activities, I began the next school year teaching language with a vengeance. I taught journal and story writing daily. We read big books, poems, and trade books, and wrote our own versions of selected ones. Different authors were studied each month. The students read each day during sustained silent reading. Our school even began a Whole Language Support Group, which I attended regularly, soaking up each new idea I could get my hands on with the determination to try them all. I continued in this frantic manner through that school year and the next as well. Because I was still teaching the basal reader, I attempted to make it more exciting by integrating whole language activities. I also became more flexible with my reading groups.

Though the classroom environment had become rich with language, there were still many stumbling blocks, inconsistencies in my teaching, and demands on my time. Our first-grade curriculum was still very skills-oriented. Not only did we use a phonics workbook, a handwriting workbook, and a spelling curriculum based on memorization, we also got a brand new basal series in 1990, complete with workbooks for each student. Our first-grade team continued to use ability grouping for reading. We created homogeneous groups, by switching classes each morning, which were then subdivided into two or three additional groups. This was the organization and methodology I knew and felt forced to use. All this, in addition to beginning a new *Math Their Way* curriculum that year, caused my energy and commitment to the whole language philosophy to ebb.

The next few years did bring some significant steps toward progress. We finally stopped switching classrooms for reading instruction and we adopted McCracken's *Spelling Through Phonics* (1982) as our primary phonics program. In 1992 and 1993, our team created two integrated themes based on winter and insects which we taught "basal-free" for a month each. As recently as 1994, we did away with our formal spelling curriculum at the first-grade level.

Each of these changes individually felt like a true progression in instruction. The problem was that each also had its own set of problems and concerns. If we do not group children by ability for reading, how can we possibly meet all of the student needs? Should I teach handwriting along with the new phonics program or stick with the handwriting workbook? If I do not use the basal for two separate months to accommodate the new themes, how will I finish all the first-grade reading books? And without a formal spelling curriculum, how do I teach students to be accountable for their spelling? All of these weighty issues put together with the everyday "whats" and "hows" caused my head to spin.

Overwhelmed and Afraid

Teachers feel a great responsibility to their students to give them the best education possible. This responsibility can be overwhelming in and of itself. We put a great deal of pressure on ourselves, and our self-confidence can be easily shaken. Often an apprehension or resistance to change occurs. I have often felt this apprehension during my career.

Ridley (1990) has identified four issues that impact teachers with regard to quality whole language instruction. First, Ridley suggests an orientation to activities versus philosophy is prevalent. This is the trap into which I have fallen. With the number of changes and additions I have instituted over the past nine years, not to mention my lack of experience prior to the "whole language revolution," I have found myself without a clear sense of my own philosophy of what is important in language instruction. Regie Routman redefines whole language in her recent book, *Literacy at the Crossroads: Crucial Talking About Reading, Writing, and Other Teaching Dilemmas:*

> *Whole language is a way of thinking, teaching, and learning in a social community where learners are continually supported to purposefully use language (reading, writing, speaking, listening, viewing, thinking, drawing, composing, making sense mathematically and scientifically, and so on) in order to inquire and to construct and evaluate their own understanding of texts and real-world issues (Routman, 1996, p. 41).*

To be able to clearly define, or redefine, one's philosophy, equal amounts of experience and information are needed. Prior to this point, I did not have the experience. Perhaps now I am ready.

A second issue Ridley (1990) reports is teachers' resistance to change. The most common type of resistance was characterized by those who added the whole language activities onto the traditional skills activities they were already using, but did not adopt the philosophy. This description characterizes my teaching methods. So it is true. I am not alone.

It is important to note that the resistance may not be a personal one. Rather, it could be administrative, parental, curricular, or peer-related resistance. In my situation, when the primary focus of a program and a professional team of colleagues is based on sequential and isolated skill and drill methodology, transitions into whole language can be even more difficult.

A completely different viewpoint may be that it is not resistance at all that holds us back. It may be fear. Some very real fears I face are:

- the unknown.
- educationally harming my students.
- not being able to meet individual needs.
- missing essential lessons in a search for authentic teaching.
- the amount of time and effort it would require.
- knowing the "whats" but not the "hows."
- teaching first graders with texts having no controlled vocabulary.
- changing assessment procedures.

While I know these fears are normal and rational, I am not sure all of them should be overcome, because they provide one basis for reflective teaching.

A third issue Ridley (1990) cites is the lack of resources for staff development. I have had training in whole language during a few summer workshops as well as a week-long after school class with Bob and Marlene McCracken. In addition, our district provided a small number of in-service days on the subject. Also, our Whole Language Support Group served as a resource. All of these, while certainly worthwhile for the information and activities, did not succeed in recreating philosophies. They all occurred during the years 1989 through 1991, and general interest diminished after that. Very few of my fellow teachers ever completely made the transition. Routman (1996, p. 38) observes that "when we are talking about a major philosophical and pedagogical shift, we need lots and lots of time, professional development, and continuous support and knowledge."

Finally, Ridley (1990) reports that teachers are concerned about accountability. Holistic instruction is based on a completely different set of outcomes than our current norm-based tests are designed to assess. While there are many assessments that can be used within a whole language classroom, they are very time consuming and do not coincide with our report cards.

Our report cards have been altered over time as well. But evolution is a slow process. Nine years ago we were still grading our first graders with letter grades (As, Bs, Cs, and so on). Since then we have changed to E, S, and I—and more recently, just S and I. Grades used to be given for all subject areas, including handwriting, reading, language, and spelling. Now we give one language arts grade with comprehension, vocabulary, spelling, handwriting, and phonics listed below as areas of concern.

The many constraints teachers feel, coupled with the large responsibility we have, cause even the most educated, dedicated professionals to be bewildered. As John C. Manning, professor at the University of Minnesota and former president of the International Reading Association said, "these classroom teachers, like so many in generations before, find themselves in a maelstrom of contradictory and intense reading curriculum opinion and bias that breeds professional self-doubt and instructional debilitation" (Manning, 1995, p. 652).

In Search of Balance

In the last two years, my motivation for new language activities and ideas has stagnated. I feel like a saturated sponge that needs to be wrung out. But into which sink? Some of my previous programs had great beginnings, but have been left by the wayside without further development. But there are some areas that have never been let go—those that have never gotten much past the traditional methods of old. It is these areas that are of major concern to me.

The use of the basal in reading instruction has frustrated me since I discovered other methods. Basal readers, probably because of their controlled text, are often boring and difficult to consider authentic literature. They can, nevertheless, suck a teacher into an imposing whirlpool of dependency. Though I do not teach phonics or language skills in conjunction with the basal, the sequential introduction of vocabulary produces a notion of being required to do every story in order. Though this may be a false assumption, the feeling is real and at times resented. On the other hand, using "literature anthologies" such as the basal, with easy vocabulary that builds on itself, gives many beginning readers a better chance of reading the material with fluency and comprehension. That has been my goal as a reading teacher.

This debate is going on among the authorities in education as well. Manning (1995) has very definite ideas of what a grade one reading program should look like. He says instruction should be strictly based on learning rate and reading instructional level through the use of controlled vocabulary and text. Therefore, he feels intraclassroom grouping is essential. Furthermore, the basal, despite its flaws, has a purpose in reading instruction, and many beginning readers actually need it to succeed, according to Manning. On the other side of the issue, Dorothy Strickland (1995) writes almost nothing about basals in her article about balanced literacy programs. The one suggestion she does give is to tear them apart and use them for student-run discussion groups. Offering a more balanced stance, Regie Routman says that when using a basal series, the teacher should be selective in the stories that are used and involve students in authentic responses to literature, including discussion groups and related author studies (Routman, 1996). Routman has always been, and still is, a proponent of holistic instruction; however, she too, is responding now to the call for balance.

Phonics and spelling are two other skills-oriented areas with which I have been disgruntled over the years. Decoding, though not reading, is a necessary reading strategy to teach. I even feel it should have some sequence and therefore necessitates isolated minilessons. Its application as a strategy should be done in the context of authentic literature and in reading or writing processes. It is easy, however, to get caught up in using skill and drill techniques that are completely disengaged from real purposes, especially when it comes to independent practice.

The formal spelling curriculum in our district has been eliminated from the first grade. This is not to say that concerns for correct spelling in writing have also been eliminated. We use invented spelling and hope for reasonable transfer of phonemic awareness in their writing. Though my students make great gains over the school year, there is currently not enough accountability for words they should know how to spell. This challenge is a monumental one when dealing with children's writing. Despite the information given at our parent-teacher open house in the fall, it continues to be an issue that concerns many of the parents.

Again, the authorities and researchers have differing views of proper skill instruction in the classroom. Manning (1995, p. 654) claims that "the amount of skill instruction in elementary school reading programs is excessive and absurd. Learning to read for many children is made proportionately more difficult with every added skill."

In that same vein, Richgels, Poremba, and McGee (1996) suggest that while direct instruction in phonemic awareness is the popular answer today, it can better be developed through holistic contexts. Dorothy Strickland (1995) also says that the basic skills should be approached through application in invented spelling and decoding in context. Routman states that phonics is the least important cueing system, and that the teaching of phonics should be strategically done in the meaningful context of the predictable stories children read and write every day (Routman, 1991). She does, however, go on to suggest a possible sequence of emphasis for teaching letter-sound relationships in the early grades. Interestingly, she puts all consonants, digraphs, and blends ahead of the vowels. Even more surprisingly, the long vowels are listed before the short vowel sounds. On the other hand, McCracken's (1982) sequence initially presents several consonants and then intersperses a new short vowel sound between each new group of consonants. The long vowels are taught once all the consonants and short vowels have been introduced. This process allows for small words to be formed by the students early on, therefore applying their phonemic awareness in a real context.

At the other side of the pendulum, current research shows that phonemic awareness training is significant to reading and writing achievement. In one study at the University of Auckland in New Zealand, five year olds were studied in whole language classrooms. One group was given phonemic awareness training, another group categorized words semantically, and a third group received no special instruction. It was found that on all measures of reading and spelling, the group with the phonemic awareness training did better than the other two groups. Keith Stanovich, a professor of applied psychology at the University of Toronto, adds that phonics and phonological awareness training help reading comprehension, not just letter and word recognition (Diegmueller, 1996a).

Many educators and researchers agree that systematic phonics and phonemic awareness lessons are necessary for that bottom percentage of children—some say five percent, others say as many as 20 percent to 30 percent—to read and write successfully. I ask, "Aren't we responsible for educating all students in our classrooms? And, therefore, shouldn't we provide the strategies necessary for all children to learn to read and write?"

Spelling also requires balanced instruction. Balance in this area seems to have been characterized by direct memorization and pure luck. Rather, the balance should be between allowing students to do a great amount of writing and expecting that certain high frequency words be spelled correctly (Routman, 1996).

Relieved, Renewed, and Ready to Juggle

The struggles in my mind, my heart, and my classroom over the years to provide the best education possible for my students are not uncommon. This is why the term "balance" in reading instruction is such a relief. It doesn't mean that we can all stop working toward the most effective reading and language curriculum, but that some pressure is relieved with regard to the battle within. The truth is, we are all in search of the same results, and all of us are right some of the time. Students and their needs are very different—from child to child, classroom to classroom, and school to school. We are professionals, and as such, we know what different students require to learn. The notion of balance is empowering, too.

With this relief comes a sense of renewal. When motivation diminishes, one's overall attitude can take on an unenthusiastic or even negative tone, which cannot help but be transferred to students. While I am sure this is a normal occurrence from time to time in a teaching career, holding on to it for too long can damage the teaching process. Renewal is essential, and the resulting effects are very motivating.

So with all this said, now what? The reevaluation of my goals for a quality language program is essential. Without it, I would simply add more activities to an already very crowded schedule. At this point in my career, these are my beliefs about and goals for the development of language learners:

- I want my students to love all kinds of literature as much as I do.

- Language should be taught through every strategy possible.

- Reading instruction for many beginning first graders needs to include use of controlled text and vocabulary.

- Skills should be taught in context wherever possible and be viewed as just one strategy in reading for fluency and comprehension.

- Many beginning first graders need sequential minilessons in phonemic awareness to jump start their reading and writing capabilities.

- Students need in-class time to read and enjoy books of their choice.

- Writing should have equal emphasis with reading in language instruction and it should be done for authentic purposes.

- Students should be held accountable for skills learned.

- All people need a great deal of modeling in order to learn—not only through the teaching process but through the emulation of role models as well.

- The greatest amount of learning takes place when it is self-motivated.

- Instruction should meet each student's needs and be at his or her level. Therefore, flexible ability groups are occasionally necessary.

- Parents should be continuously and diligently involved in their children's learning and should also serve as instructional role models.

My current reading/language arts program already includes most of these beliefs, but at times it does not seem in balance.

Conclusion

My evolution from a "skill and drill" reading teacher, through the explosion of whole language, and a "do it all" mentality that caused overwhelming anxiety, to the search for balance and renewal has been both frustrating and exciting. The students have continually given me the reason to move forward. They take what I give them and do their best, even when I know there has to be a better way to reach them all.

And so these nine years of experience and growth have helped me to put the puzzle pieces of language together. Children love a completed puzzle. When a piece is taken off, they will attend to it as long as they soon see it put back again to form the whole picture. I am now a somewhat older and wiser, highly motivated teacher of the whole balanced language puzzle.

A Third-Grade Teacher's Vision of Balanced Reading Instruction

Loria Thatcher

The term "balanced reading instruction" is beginning to gain popularity as teachers, administrators, community members, and other stakeholders have seen problems in the ways that some students are being taught today. All students are unique. With this knowledge, the concept of a balanced reading program just makes good sense to many of us in the classroom.

Balanced reading instruction refers to the daily balance or integration of strategies and skills within meaningful contexts both in the classroom and outside it. Some students need to be taught skills that other students inherently seem to know, perhaps because of intellectual ability or environmental-socioeconomic advantages. Parents, practices, and practitioners are all part of the balance that we as teachers are seeking to create. The 3 P's of balance are interrelated and one cannot exist without the others.

As many buzz words used in the history of reading instruction are being scrutinized, I believe that the term "balanced reading instruction" is not in danger of generating similar controversy. The term "balance" doesn't lend itself to any bandwagon trends. The balance of instruction and/or philosophy does not imply only one right way to do something. Balance is a halfway point, a compromise, wherein teachers balance strategies, skills, and approaches to meet students' needs.

Reasons Influencing a Need for Balance

The following are some of the many reasons that a balanced reading program is needed:

1. *Readers need phonic knowledge.*
   Students need a variety of word identification strategies when they encounter unknown words. Such strategies include the use of context, the flow of language, and the structure of words. If students do not have basic phonic knowledge, they will be unable to use these strategies in tandem, which is a characteristic of effective readers.

2. *Students need to know and use spelling strategies, rules, and/or generalizations.*
   Although the English language is somewhat inconsistent in spelling, some of the more basic strategies should be taught. In order for students to make connections between known words and new words, spelling patterns should be pointed out to them within the context of real acts of reading. I am not advocating that teachers give explicit lessons on lists of words that all have the same rules and/or generalizations, but I am proposing that whichever ways teachers decide to handle language arts programs, children need to know the way words work. Using the book *Making Big Words* (Cunningham & Hall, 1994a) is a great thematic, multilevel way to incorporate phonics and spelling skills into the classroom.

3. *Students need to be asked to do more higher level thinking.*
   Although knowing basic factual information is necessary to comprehend a story, too many low-level questions are being asked in classrooms. In today's society, citizens are faced with many problems in the workplace and their personal lives. In order to better prepare students for what they will encounter in the real world, we need to arm them with some strong critical thinking skills. Being able to synthesize facts and ideas, interpret character actions, and apply knowledge is of utmost importance.

4. *Students need word recognition strategies.*
   In my classroom last year, many students arrived either having forgotten or not knowing any word recognition strategies besides sounding words out from the initial phoneme to the final phoneme. It became clear to me that this was causing many of my students to get stumped while reading, and they could not find their way out of the problem. I began to do more modeling, thinking aloud, and reading aloud than I had done the previous year,

and I focused on teaching students the strategies needed for word recognition, which helped their comprehension. It worked!

5. *Students learn by different means or modes.*
   Because students learn differently, no one approach to teaching can be used with success for all students. Some students are visual learners, some are tactile learners, some are more kinesthetic, etc. Students need to be taught in a number of ways in order to meet their needs.

Major Areas Characterizing Balance

In this section, I will share seven statements that I feel are most important to remember when trying to create a balanced reading program in your school or classroom.

1. *Within the context of "real reading" situations, students need to be taught reading skills.*
   Examples for third grade include the following: using context, cause and effect, fact and opinion, survey or preview, and categorizing. What I mean by "real reading" is that these skills can be taught while reading a book that is integrated into what is already going on in the classroom. It isn't necessary to use isolated skill worksheets all the time.

2. *Within the context of "real reading" situations, students need to be taught word recognition strategies.*
   I heard Wanda Lincoln speak at the Northern Illinois Reading Conference a few years ago. She shared some phrases that I then copied, posted in my room, and referred to often. The poster is shown in Figure 1.1.

   These are the strategies that my third graders have had great success in using. "Skip it" refers to putting a blank in place of the unknown word and rereading the sentence using context clues to try to figure out the meaning of the unknown word. "Break it" refers to examining the word for any little words within the larger word. When students see word parts that they can pronounce or read, usually they can put the rest of the sounds and the context of the sentence together to figure out what the word means. "Frame it" means to look at the word alone. The student can then

Figure 1.1: Strategies to Use When You Come to an Unknown Word

1. Skip it.
2. Break it.
3. Frame it.
4. Sound it.
5. Ask.

determine if he or she has ever seen the word before. If so, where? Pictures can also be used for clues during this step. "Sound it" refers to sounding out a word. This strategy, if used before the others, usually won't work as well. In my classroom experience, it is the combination of these steps that help students with comprehension. If all else fails and they still can't tell what the unknown word is, they may "ask" me. I will then give them a choice of a few words that they can choose from. This helps them feel that they are responsible for figuring out the word. If students are not taught these strategies, or any one strategy is over-used, some students will struggle. I have included book-marks I use in my classroom. The bookmarks help students remember the important strategies they can use to figure out unknown words.

3. *Students need to be social in their attempts with reading in order to become lifelong readers and learners.*
   Literature circles, debates, discussions, and critical thinking need to take place in order for reading to become something that children genuinely want to do. As adults, we know that when we read a great book, we don't want to keep it to ourselves. We want to share our opinion, thoughts, and reflections with others. When we allow students to discuss what they are reading, the act and process of reading becomes a more purposeful and enjoyable thing to do. It then becomes more authentic.

4. *Spelling should be an integrated part of the existing curriculum and not taught as a separate subject.*
   Spelling rules and generalizations need to be taught and words need to be used in meaningful contexts, not with an

Figure 1.2: Bookmarks

Tips for Unknown Words for the
Reader

1. Look at the picture

2. Think about what would make sense.

3. Read the sentence again and get your mouth ready.

4. Skip the word and read on.

  Try to use context (clues) in the sentence to help you figure out the word.

5. Try to say more than the beginning letter. Look for chunks you know.

6. Ask for help.

Tips and Prompts for the
Listener

Wait - Allow discovery time (5 to 10 seconds)

When the reader is having difficulty, say the following:

"Look at the picture."

- or -

"What would make sense?"

- or -

"Read it again and get your mouth ready."

- or -

"Skip that word and read on. Can you use the context of the sentence to help you figure out the word?"

- or -

"Is it _____ or _____?" (Give the reader a choice.)

• Not all errors need to be corrected. If an error changes the meaning of the sentence, say: "Try that again."

isolated list that has nothing to do with what else is going on in the classroom. Word lists can be generated in a number of different ways, according to teacher philosophy and available resources.

5. *When worksheets are used, they should involve real acts of reading, not isolated skills.*
   If worksheets or skill sheets aren't connected to what is being studied in the classroom, many children have trouble carrying over skills and using them in authentic contexts after the worksheet is finished. There are good worksheets out there, but teachers must take care in choosing these materials. Worksheets that are more open-ended and less "fill-in-the-blank" types are most beneficial to meeting the needs of struggling students and challenging those who are more able.

6. *The five years prior to school are very important for literacy development. Parents are their children's first teachers and need to be involved as much as possible.*
   Parents should be kept well informed, given ideas, and invited to school. Some teachers have an easier time involving parents than others. Parents are one of the "Ps" of balance. We want all parties to work together cohesively to balance the reading program.

7. *Assessments should be both informal and formal in nature.*
   Informal devices, such as an informal reading inventory, are extremely beneficial in trying to figure out where a child is along the continuum and what the next learning step for that child is. Formal measures, such as standardized tests, do a good or adequate job of measuring a child's growth from year to year, or of comparing schools to one another. In order to become informed about a child, both types of measures must be used. Not all standardized tests give a true picture of what a student knows, and not all informal measures do either. Balance, again, is the key.

All of these elements of a balanced reading program are equally important. Each one works with the next while we learn that there is no such thing as "the way" to teach all students.

Closing Comments

Last year, I taught third grade in Plainfield, Illinois. I had a class of 31 children. Of these 31 students, three received speech services, three received learning disability services, three took Ritalin for Attention Deficit Disorder, and three were enrolled in the district's gifted education program. At the beginning of the year, several of my students were reading well below grade level, while several were reading well above. With this many students of varying skill and ability levels, I knew I needed to employ many strategies to attempt to meet the needs of all of my students.

Parents are just as much a part of the balance as are my practices and skills as a classroom teacher. All three must work together. None can succeed effectively without the others. The most important thing to ask yourself each day is, "Am I doing everything I can to meet the needs of all of the children?" If your answer to yourself each day is "yes," then I believe that you have a balanced reading program.

As a classroom teacher, I have struggled to pull it all together to meet the needs of my many diverse learners. Hopefully, the teachers' voices in this book will help you better understand your own philosophy while you begin to make some changes in practice, if necessary. We don't propose that we have all of the answers. After all, if we did, we would have "the way," but teaching is just not that simple.

Narrowing the Focus

In this section, we begin to narrow the focus to see what balanced reading instruction looks like within specific classroom contexts. The two articles in this section provide an overview of the major components of a balanced literacy curriculum and how they function within the classroom. These articles explore the roles of developmental, functional, and recreational components of reading and writing. In addition, they address the need for balancing shared, guided, and independent reading and writing activities within the classroom. As you read this section, we urge you to consider how these authors' ideas about the major components of balanced reading instruction compare with your own ideas and experiences.

The Reality of Balanced Literacy in a Primary Classroom

Jenelle Gallagher-Mance

The concept of balance is one of the essential ingredients conducive to the existence of all living and nonliving things: the balance of a region's ecosystem, the balance of our country's budget, the physical balance of a toddler as he or she begins to walk, and the balance of nutritional foods in one's diet. Maintaining a sense of balance is a struggle and a challenge that many people encounter on a daily basis. For example, many working mothers attempt to balance career, family, education, friendship, and personal growth. On a daily basis, the media continues to highlight dangerous individuals who often correlate their imbalance of love and guidance during their childhoods to their unspeakable acts of violence today.

Educational researchers and professionals have bombarded the field with a wealth of new, updated, and refined theory and research. Many teachers are eager to put these ideas into practice but become discouraged due to lack of administrative, community, and political support. In addition, as the pendulum swings from skills-based to whole language instruction, many teachers have become frustrated and confused. To counteract the pendulum swings in reading education, many educators are calling for balance in reading instruction.

Theoretical Foundations

The whole language movement has become a source of controversy as many classroom teachers attempt to balance its strengths with more traditional approaches. Brian Cambourne's (1988) conditions of learning have provided a sound theoretical base for the whole language movement. Cambourne identifies eight essential elements for successful and effective learning to occur: immersion, expectation, responsibility, approximation, demonstration, use, feedback, and engagement. Similarly, Don Holdaway (1979) presents four factors that require balance in order to establish a literacy set. The factors include motivational, linguistic, operational, and orthographic elements.

New Zealand's extremely high literacy rate has captured reading professionals' attention. Through the work and philosophy of Marie Clay, the founder of the successful Reading Recovery program, teachers have been challenged to rethink the way they teach reading. Clay (1979) proposed the use of several important guidelines that contribute to the overall effectiveness of a reading program. These guidelines provide the form for individualized early intervention. Such instruction is consistent with specific student goals, and the student reads and rereads materials at his or her instructional level. During the process of reading connected text, the student is directly taught a core of metacognitive strategies based on semantic, syntactic, and graphophonic cueing systems. Writing is an integral part of the program, with an emphasis on phonemic awareness. Congruency between these interventions and the classroom reading program becomes essential in order for the student to apply his or her learning to new situations (Spiegel, 1995).

The capacity of educational research to enhance instructional methods depends upon the professional to accurately and efficiently put theory into practice. Today, educators are faced with a very diverse student population, which makes the concept of balance critical. How does a balanced literacy program look in practice? How does the balance reflect the developmental level of the students? How does the classroom teacher maintain balance in his or her own life during this professional challenge? In this article, I will present my first-grade classroom in order to identify the components and rationale of a balanced literacy program.

Components of Balanced Literacy in First Grade

Because of current educational structures, the notion of balanced reading in any classroom will often look quite different from year to year, due to the students involved. The varying and diverse needs of the students can greatly affect the perspectives and philosophies of the educator. A reformed curriculum based on administrative decisions and the varying effects and voices of the school community have a dramatic impact on today's classrooms. Each of the vital components influences the governing elements and purposes of a sound reading program: developmental, functional, and recreational.

Developmental reading instruction usually receives heavy emphasis in first grade due to the overall purpose of learning to read. Functional literacy is developed through components that encourage students to read in order to learn. Recreational reading guides the affective aspect of student learning, with a focus on positive attitudes and the pleasure of the reading act. It is a professional challenge to maintain a delicate and essential balance in my first-grade classroom. The daily instructional components that I use include literacy play, read-alouds, language experience, shared reading, shared writing, vocabulary experience, guided reading, guided writing, spelling, independent reading, and independent writing.

Literacy Play

Literacy play involves play activities that are organized to enhance functional literacy development in an incidental way. No direct instruction is provided; however, the situation is organized in such a way as to encourage reading, writing, vocabulary, listening, and speaking as a natural by-product of the activity (Morrow, 1993). Specific materials used as literacy props must be available and students must be encouraged to interact with those materials. For example, a kitchen play center will include both props and functional printed materials, such as telephone books, a real telephone, emergency number decals, cookbooks, blank recipe cards, empty grocery containers, food coupons, grocery store ads, notepads, pens, pencils, and markers. These items are incorporated into the students' informal dramatic play. An advanced form of literacy play can be promoted through literacy centers, such as reading, spelling, drama, listening, computer, and writing centers. This essential interaction with language can be achieved through word games, flannel boards, puppetry, overhead projectors with transparencies of poems, and old filmstrip projectors. Literacy play is encouraged by a print-rich environment, including a well-stocked quality classroom library and a wealth of supplies, such as paper, pencils, magnetic letters, chalkboards, typewriters, and envelopes that encourage written and oral communication.

Read-Alouds

The read-aloud component promotes and develops recreational, functional, and developmental literacy through demonstration. Author Jim Trelease (1989) exclaims in *The New Read-Aloud Handbook* that "Reading aloud is the best advertisement because it works" (p. 9). It allows children to sample the delights of reading. It also conditions them to believe that reading is a pleasurable experience. Reading aloud to children should always be valued. It should be seen as a special activity, a worthwhile way to spend time, and a shared pleasure, which should have a prominent place in the daily program at all ages (*Guided Reading*, 1995). Storytelling adds another dimension to the read-aloud component, by developing aspects such as entertainment, empowerment, and education (Horner, 1996). Storytelling can take many forms. In my first-grade classroom, the students enjoy visual representations of a story through the use of a velcro storytelling apron. Pictures of characters, settings, and props are simply attached to the apron as the story is told. Stories told with the use of real props, such as a scarf or stuffed animal, quickly capture the students' attention.

Language Experience

The developmental component can be fulfilled through the use of language experience. In a balanced literacy program, many opportunities are provided for students to participate in hands-on experiences such as cooking, art projects, math activities, and science experiments. The language generated from these activities is recorded by the teacher during a group or individual writing activity. Because of its relevance and the fact that it is recorded in the children's own words, the text produced is highly predictable and readable for the students (*Guided Reading*, 1995).

Shared Reading

Shared reading welcomes all students to the literacy club by providing them with lively and enjoyable reading experiences where success is guaranteed. Shared reading is based on the bedtime reading experience. It involves the teacher with a whole class sitting close together while they share in the reading and rereading of appealing rhymes, songs, poems, and stories (*Guided Reading*, 1995). I also use shared reading as an opportunity to expose students to a variety of genres, such as nonfiction, historical fiction, fairy tales, folk tales, and biographies. Advanced shared reading may include book selections for explicit skill and strategy instruction on topics such as quotation marks, sight words, self-monitoring, and prior knowledge.

Shared Writing

Shared writing builds on the developmental model of reading instruction. Just as reading to students models reading behavior, writing in front of students models writing behavior. As the teacher writes, he or she thinks out loud, sharing the thought process involved while writing and inviting the students to contribute. Opportunities arise in all the content areas for teachers to write in front of students throughout the day (*Guided Reading*, 1995). Shared writing experiences should parallel the students' stages of writing development. As students demonstrate understandings and skills, the shared writing experience should include explicit instruction specific to the students' strengths and weaknesses.

Vocabulary

A sound reading program continues to evolve through the inclusion of vocabulary experiences which enhance functional literacy. The vocabulary experiences that exist in the classroom should include not just one interaction with a word, but many interactions with words in various contexts. Varied contexts such as picture dictionaries, word walls, graphic organizers, word play, focus lessons, and guided discussion should gradually build the student's level of understanding regarding new words (Paynter & Marzano, 1992). For example, in a first-grade classroom, word play may include the daily reading of jokes and riddles collected in a "joke basket."

Guided Reading

Guided reading is carried out in small, relatively homogeneous groups. The teacher provides students with supportive text and facilitates a discussion of the story which enables the students to feel capable and confident of reading the text independently. The purpose of guided reading is to provide a confirming experience for the readers and to provide an opportunity for the teacher to observe, monitor, and coach (*Guided Reading*, 1995). Critical thinking about content and the self-monitoring of reading strategies and decoding skills becomes the core of guided reading.

Guided Writing

Likewise, guided writing is the heart of the developmental writing program. It takes place when students have time to write and the teacher is available for guidance. Guided writing, like guided reading, occurs after students have had many opportunities to see writing demonstrated on the chalkboard and the overhead projector in shared contexts (*Guided Reading*, 1995). The teacher also conducts explicit lessons which demonstrate the stages of the writing process. Graphic organizers develop organization of ideas, and individual writing conferences with the teacher and classroom volunteers provide essential support for young writers. Opportunities to share published works from an author's chair (a designated place for young writers to sit when they orally share their writing with the class) build positive attitudes and a sense of accomplishment.

Spelling

Explicit and direct instruction in spelling strategies and skills is a vital component of any literacy program. Phonemic awareness, word building, and decoding are used to establish avenues of successful spelling with beginning writers. For example, a class of first graders may collectively generate lists of rhyming words based on word patterns. A systematic approach to phonics instruction during the emergent stages of literacy especially enables the struggling reader to decode unknown words in conjunction with multiple strategies. Weekly spelling tests based on frequently used sight words balances direct instruction with application. Effective phonics instruction also takes place during shared and guided reading activities. The graphophonic cueing system is developed in conjunction with other strategies. Teacher comments such as, "Check the first two letters. What word would make sense using those sounds?" demonstrate the application of phonic knowledge for young readers.

Independent Reading

Independent reading is an extremely important, integral part of a balanced literacy program wherein students choose to read and enjoy reading for the pleasure of doing so (*Guided Reading*,

1995). Silent reading time, such as "Drop Everything and Read!" (DEAR), becomes a daily routine for helping readers synthesize and apply their strategies and skills independently. In addition, books that have been successfully used during the guided reading component are then available for students to read and share with families at home.

Independent Writing

The students' independent writing completes the components of a balanced literacy program. As an adult writer composes, reviews, thinks, and often reworks a piece several times— so do children as they participate in writing as a process (*Guided Reading*, 1995). In my first-grade classroom, students have multiple opportunities to conference with an adult in order to edit and finally publish their writing. During these conferences, I provide explicit instruction on conventions of writing, spelling patterns, and other aspects of written language. Students publish their writing and illustrations in homemade books. Published books are housed in our classroom library for repeated readings. The students also reinforce their phonic understandings as they write for their own purposes and self-select their own topics. Independent writing will often be observed during informal dramatic play episodes or during the rough draft stage of the writing process.

Degree of Emphasis

Satisfying a delicate sense of balance among the various components of a reading program can be frustrating and confusing. The degree of emphasis for each component is largely dependent upon student needs and stages of literacy development (Paynter & Marzano, 1992).

Readers and writers at the emergent stage are developing an awareness of print, some letter/sound associations, attitudes toward reading, and listening comprehension skills. Children profit from daily experiences with literacy play, read-alouds, language experience, shared reading, shared writing, vocabulary experience, and phonics instruction.

The beginning stage of literacy finds readers and writers generally applying phonic skills to their writing, developing a sense of the multiple strategies used during reading, and successfully reading books with rhyme and repetition. Components such as read-alouds, guided reading, guided writing, vocabulary experience, spelling, and phonics build upon the beginning reader's strengths while continuing to guide the learner toward independence. Fluent readers and writers naturally use multiple strategies in conjunction with efficient self-monitoring for successful and accurate literacy experiences.

In a balanced reading program, heavy emphasis should be placed on components such as read-alouds, vocabulary experience, independent reading, independent writing, and spelling in order to foster self-reliance as readers synthesize and critically evaluate text. A variety of instructional groupings can be used in order to match appropriate instruction with specific student needs, thus evolving into a sense of balance.

Personal Struggles

The overall success of any instructional program begins with the classroom teacher. A variety of personal struggles will often accompany the educator as he or she copes with the complexity of a balanced reading program. Issues such as staff collegiality, communication with parents, teacher self-confidence, and attitude can have dramatic impact on the effectiveness of the classroom teacher. Collaboration, sharing, and support among staff members, particularly at the same grade level, not only provide teachers with a wealth of new ideas, but will considerably lighten the work load, support the novice colleague, and create the best possible solutions to the many problems that arise daily.

Teacher self-confidence and attitude must be consistently focused on the positive. The wealth of new research and instructional methods makes it tempting for the educator to set a goal of enthusiastically "doing it all" within a short period of time. I am learning the importance of accepting my mistakes, learning from them, and setting realistic goals within the confines of a six-and-a-half hour teaching day. A professional sense of accountability must be maintained through a commitment to student learning. The concept of "less is often much more" needs to be balanced with a willingness to take a risk. I often find myself attempting too many new ideas at once, creating much more frustration than accomplishment. The profession needs to move forward with decisions based on careful consideration. How many times have educators embraced a new approach only to later discover its lack of merit?

Parents who are well-informed and enthusiastically welcomed into the school environment can provide important connections and balance between school and home learning. Parent education programs that promote instructional information, family literacy, or even effective parenting strategies help to solidify school-community relationships. My colleagues and I are developing a series of parent information sessions with a focus on reading. Our goals include informing parents of recent, helpful research and the theories that underlie our literacy instruction. We also share specific activities that promote family literacy in the home environment. I am exploring other techniques that promote family literacy: an expanded classroom lending library, a writing box containing a variety of writing instruments and paper for daily checkout, and a portable listening center with a personal cassette player and headphones that allows children to listen to books at home.

Conclusion

The reality of a quality education includes a balanced reading program which may look different from classroom to classroom. Conscientious educators are empowered to make sound instructional decisions based on the careful assessment of their students. Those decisions incorporate a variety of literacy components which delicately support one another in order to maintain an essential sense of balance. Just as an unbalanced ecosystem painstakingly eliminates its inhabitants, an unbalanced education can eliminate student potential for future success and happiness.

A Balanced Reading Program in a First- and Second-Grade Classroom

Cynthia Vandergriff

I believe that whole language is a philosophy, and I value many of the methods that are stressed within this philosophy. The term whole language has been interpreted differently by many educators. Some people believe that phonics does not play an active role in the whole language program, but I disagree. I consider myself a whole language teacher, but I use whatever methods and strategies are appropriate to meet the needs of my students. I have taught first and second grades for a total of six years. For the last three years, I have been involved in a multiyear grouping situation. One year I teach first grade and the following year I move with my class to second grade. This article focuses on my efforts to achieve balance in my reading program at these two grade levels.

For some teachers and administrators, balanced reading instruction can mean different things. For me, a balanced reading program consists of developmental, functional, and recreational components. The developmental component consists of skills and strategies; the functional component focuses on reading to gain information; and the recreational component is reading for fun and pleasure. Within this framework, teachers can use a variety of strategies and methods to meet individual student's needs. There is no one best way to teach reading. It should not be purely phonics based, nor should it be based upon a purist view of whole language.

The Developmental Component

In first grade, most of my students need a strong phonics background. They need to feel comfortable with sounds and develop phonemic awareness. I teach phonics through the use of literature, and I only isolate instruction for those students who need extra reinforcement. My classroom is very student-centered and my students have many opportunities to read a variety of different genres of literature. Good literature makes it possible to have meaningful discussions about what has been read. It also motivates the students to read other books by the same author or from the same genre.

Our first-grade reading program is literature-based, and we are fortunate enough to have multiple copies of many fine pieces of literature to support this program. Our program consists of teaching skills and strategies, student research, recreational reading, and many opportunities for written expression.

I usually teach by using certain themes: seasons, holidays, animal habitats, and the Arctic. Our literature ties into all of these areas. Author studies are also an important part of our curriculum; Norman Bridwell, Frank Asch, and Eric Carle are some of our favorites. Generally, I introduce a book to the whole class, and then we participate in many pre-reading activities, such as word sorts, probable passages, word chains, possible sentences, and word maps. After I read the story to the whole group, they usually want to read the story with a partner. If the material is too difficult for some of the students, I pair them with a more able reader. I feel very strongly about sharing books with the whole class; I do not feel it is appropriate for students to be told they cannot read a book. If the material is too difficult, I give those children more experiences with the text, such as: recording the story on tape, sending it home to read with parents, storytelling that particular story to a small group, or having older students or parent volunteers read it to individual students. The students feel more comfortable in the whole group setting when they are familiar with the text. I have not found this approach a hindrance, and it has been beneficial to less able readers.

After reading the text with the whole class, students are ready to break into flexible small groups. These groups can be structured by ability, interest, or friendship. The purpose of these groups is to discuss the text and to promote critical thinking. Whatever the case may be, I try to meet the students' needs in the small groups or on an individual basis. When students are grouped by their needs, I can introduce new strategies or skills. The small group setting is more conducive to learning a particular skill. I feel that it is important and meaningful for students when

I introduce phonics through the literature. We are very fortunate to have many books to accomplish this in a thematic way.

In my first grade, formal and informal assessments are used to determine students' strengths and weaknesses. The *Gates-MacGinitie Reading Tests* (MacGinitie & MacGinitie, 1989) are given as the formal measure. This test focuses on vocabulary and comprehension and measures general reading achievement. I believe that using one test only gives me a small picture of a student's strengths and weaknesses. I prefer to give multiple assessments that are both formal and informal in nature so that I am better able to see the child as a whole. I use *Concepts About Print* (Clay, 1993a), which evaluates what a child knows about print. This test provides insight into what children already know about print and what they still need to be taught. A reading attitude survey provides information on a child's view about reading. I prefer to use the *Elementary Reading Attitude Survey* (McKenna & Kear, 1990). This survey measures both recreational and academic attitudes about reading. I feel it is also essential to find out about my students' interests. At the beginning of the year, I use an interest inventory to find out what my students' likes and dislikes are. This information has proven to be beneficial when it comes to planning units of study.

The use of a basal series is a concern of many educators and administrators. Many people who learned how to read with a basal wonder why today should be any different. The newer basal series are much more of an anthology than they used to be. I have integrated both the basal and children's literature into our program. If I feel that a story from a basal is meaningful and worthwhile to read, then I will share it with the class in the same manner as I present a novel or a trade book. I do not read each story in the basal in sequence because I do not believe that practice is worthwhile for my students.

The Functional Component

Our themes also lend themselves to research studies. We have many books at all levels about animals and their habitats. The students begin their research by using a KWL (Ogle, 1986), a technique where they brainstorm about what they *Know*, what they *Want* to know, and what they have *Learned*. Then they research on their own or within the classroom. I find that reading for information is extremely useful even at the first-grade level.

When the students are doing research, the library provides yet another source of information. Researching a topic stimulates outside reading as well.

Recreational Component: The Love of Reading

The next component of my balanced reading program involves recreational reading. Each day, I provide 15 minutes for uninterrupted silent reading. The students are extremely excited about this time of the day. I allow them to sit anywhere in the room and choose as many books as they desire. Our first-grade team has also devised a take home backpack with a variety of books for the children to read at home with a parent. The backpack contains a response journal and a sock puppet for further extension activities. The backpack idea has been a beneficial tool in promoting outside reading and parental involvement. The first-grade students are expected to read a minimum of ten minutes nightly and to record their books in a log. These logs are collected at the end of each month.

Literature circles provide a meaningful way of grouping students according to their interests. Literature circles are heterogeneous groups of children who meet for the purpose of sharing their thoughts and feelings about books they have read (Paziotopoulos & Kroll, 1992). The groups meet to read and reflect on what they have read. Literature circles promote natural discussions that lead to critical thinking. They promote a love for literature and positive attitudes toward reading (Campbell-Hill, Johnson, & Schlick-Noe, 1995). Literature circles foster interaction and collaboration between peers and expose children to a wide variety of literature from multiple perspectives. I feel that it is important for students of all abilities to share their thoughts with each other.

Title I Children in a Balanced Reading Program

Some students in my classroom need additional reinforcement of skills. These children meet with our Title I teacher for additional services. The Title I program is also literature-based, with attention focused on word recognition, comprehension, and vocabulary development. The Title I teacher and I work very closely together and collaborate once a week. I feel that our Title

I program supports balanced reading instruction. Students are given many opportunities to read real literature and focus on strategies while simultaneously practicing phonics skills. The students review vocabulary and focus on developing phonemic awareness on a daily basis. Meeting individual needs is a top priority.

How Writing Fits in a Balanced Reading Program

Since writing is a vital part of reading, my first-grade class is given time to write every day. Daily journals, response journals, a writing center, and a writer's workshop are part of our reading program.

Journaling is an excellent tool to motivate further writing. Students keep a daily journal that they write in every morning and share each day. The students enjoy writing about their thoughts and sharing them with their peers.

The students also have reading-response journals. These journals are an important part of our reading program. The students use the journals to log in their responses to what they have read. Prompts are usually provided for the students to stimulate their thinking. Some examples are the following (Kroll & Paziotopoulos, 1993):

- Did anything in this story surprise you?
- Did the setting change throughout the story?
- On a scale of one to five, how would you rate this book? Why?
- How is the story like real life?
- How did this story make you feel?
- Would you recommend this story to a friend? Why?

We have a writing center in our classroom as well. The students are actively engaged in the writing process, and they enjoy publishing stories using the materials in our writing center. Our writing center is filled with many materials, such as writing utensils, different types of writing paper, and covers of all kinds. The students enjoy going to the center during their free time to work on their own stories and poems.

My first graders also participate in a writer's workshop. It is modified for their age, but the lessons are integrated into the time block to teach certain writing skills. The children are actively involved in pre-writing, editing, conferencing, and publishing. At the end of each school year, we invite parents to school to listen to all of our stories at our Author's Tea.

The Program in Second Grade

The three components, developmental, functional, and recreational, have proven to be very successful in creating a balanced reading program in first grade. This view of instruction is carried on to second grade with my students.

Multi-Year Grouping

I am involved in a multi-year grouping situation with my students. I take my entire first-grade class to second grade. This is beneficial in many ways: (1) it allows me the advantage of knowing the students' strengths and weaknesses; (2) it gives me the opportunity to work with those children who need a little more time; and (3) it gives the students the advantage of continuing with a teacher who uses the same teaching style.

I feel that I establish the foundation of a balanced reading program in first grade, and I am able to continue this practice in second grade. Although the materials are different and the expectations are higher, the philosophy is still the same. My goal is to provide a balance of good literature along with strategies and skills to meet the needs of all my students. Teachers today know that all students learn at different rates and in different ways. Even if you present your "best" lesson, not every student is going to understand it. I feel the best teachers are those who try many different approaches and who reflect on their successes and failures to become more effective instructors.

In addition, I feel that I have an advantage in second grade because I know my students' strengths and weaknesses. I do not need to spend a great deal of time on interest inventories or attitude surveys. When we are reading and focusing on skills and strategies, I can gather students in small groups to reinforce and review skills that were previously introduced. The students also work together to help each other solve problems. They feel close to each other, and they are not afraid to take risks.

The methods taught in second grade are very similar to those taught in first grade. The difference is in the materials and the expectations. I believe that this continuous balanced program is conducive to learning. The students are very familiar with my style, and they feel comfortable with me as well as their peers.

Summary

In summary, a balanced reading program must consist of the following: a developmental component where skills and strategies are taught; a functional component where the students are reading to gain information; and a recreational component where the students develop a love for literature and pursue it outside the classroom. Remember, it is important to meet all learners' needs, no matter what methods you use. If a balanced reading program is continuous throughout all the grade levels, the students will benefit greatly. A "balance" is proportioned, just as reading instruction should be.

3

Classroom Portraits

The goal of this section is to provide you with portraits of the many faces and facets of balanced reading instruction. The six articles in this section provide close up views of balanced reading instruction in action. Using ample detail, clear descriptions, and personal insights, the authors of these articles "paint" engaging portraits of their classrooms.

As you read these articles, you will note that the authors represent a wide variety of teaching levels and educational experiences. For example, the authors of these articles teach first grade through high school, and they teach in schools which range from progressive to traditional. Some of the teachers are required to use basals for reading instruction, and others have complete freedom to select instructional materials. Some of these authors completed their teacher education programs during times when skills-based instruction was in favor, and others learned almost exclusively about the whole language philosophy in their teacher education programs. All of these factors come into play as the authors define and describe balanced reading instruction. We believe that the multiple portraits in this section will help you begin to see how different teachers balance reading instruction.

Balanced Reading Instruction: One Teacher's Voice

Suzie Lobdell

In the teaching profession today, both new and experienced teachers struggle with the changes that are occurring in how reading is taught. Some teachers continue to teach phonics and use basal readers while others have been using whole language and trade books. Even though most of the material being used can help teach students to read, whole language or basal materials alone are not meeting all of our students' needs. Teachers know that students have different modes of learning. Some students learn very easily by reading trade books and sitting through focus lessons. They pick up the skills they need with indirect instruction and function well in a whole language classroom. Other students need the direct instruction that phonics and basal activities offer. These students need things to be pointed out to them, and they need teachers to model the behaviors that they are expected to display. These children cannot learn as well by the indirect modes of instruction. Neither of these types of learners are poor learners; they just need varying types of instruction. Since all children learn differently, and all teachers teach differently, it would benefit the learners to have as many ways as possible to learn. Therefore, I am advocating a balanced reading approach.

As adults, we need balance in all parts of our lives: between work and play, sleeping and waking, being alone and being with people, being with children and being with adults. The balanced reading approach offers a wide range of options. No longer will we just teach phonics, instruct only from trade books, or focus solely on language experience. This approach is a blend of all the good things we have done in reading. There is not just one best way to teach reading. All of us, being different people, have successfully taught students to read by various methods. "Because reading is such a complex undertaking, no one strategy works to teach reading. Rather, many useful strategies can be employed" (Depree, Bancroft, Anderson, Clay, & Giacobbe, 1990, p. 2). In an effort to reach every student, let us begin to use all of these methods that have made readers of our students.

Background

Let me begin by telling you about where I have come from to reach this understanding. I grew up in a suburban community where I learned to read by the reading group, seat-work model. I remember some students leaving my room in order to receive reading instruction by other classroom teachers, but I was not one of them. I do not remember being in either the high or low reading groups. Unlike some, I do not have a clear memory of which children were in these groups. During my elementary years, I do not remember being instructed in phonics or using a phonics workbook. I never did any process writing in grade school or junior high. Instead, I copied writing, such as stories or poems, from the chalkboard. After I graduated from high school, I attended a college located in the suburbs of a large city. During my studies, I learned about language experience charts, how to teach from a basal reader, how to use trade books in the classroom, how to make and use learning centers, and how to construct a unit or theme. I was never instructed in how to teach phonics, what the real meaning of whole language was, or how to adequately assess students.

Experience

I received my first teaching job right out of college. I began teaching second grade in a private inner-city school to mostly bilingual, Hispanic students. I did not speak Spanish. At this school, everyone had reading at the same time. Since most of my second graders were reading at a first-grade level, I taught first-grade reading. (I am not suggesting that all inner-city children are reading at a low level, but merely commenting on the fact that these students were a little behind their grade level because they had to first become proficient in a second language.)

Because the whole school had reading at the same time, teachers were able to interchange students and teach only two or three levels. Another teacher taught high second-grade readers and low third-grade readers, while I instructed average and low second-grade readers, along with high first-grade readers. During this time, we also used seat-work, phonics instruction, and copying writing from the board. Phonics was explicitly taught and a phonics workbook was used every day. As I said earlier, I had neither learned by the phonics method nor was instructed as to how to teach it. I learned the sounds, reasons, and rules right along with my first class. I remember thinking, "Wow! That's why that word sounds like that!" Even though I was an excellent student, an avid reader, and a college graduate, the mysteries of print were still being unlocked for me as an adult. I found myself wishing that I had been taught these rules in elementary school because they made so much sense to me now. As I began to understand the importance of phonics, I really stressed it during this time in my teaching career. During my first two years, I had 18 and 19 students respectively. I also wanted to incorporate what I had learned from my college years by doing some cooperative learning and center time. Unfortunately, the principal, whose office was right under my classroom, felt that students who were working hard in school and learning a lot were students who worked quietly in their seats. This made it hard to teach the way I had dreamed about in college.

My third year of teaching began with 36 students! Also, this year the principal decided that we had too many low readers. To alleviate this problem, she decided that students would no longer be changing rooms for reading unless they were moving up. Each teacher would now have to instruct his or her own class. Everyone had to begin that fall with reading materials that were designated for their grade level. Suddenly, I had to instruct twice as many students, most of whom were one grade level behind in reading, and I was only allowed to use second-grade material. I changed to whole class instruction for skills and used groups for reading time. I still tried to use some learning centers, but I was mostly teaching through workbooks, phonics pages, silent reading, handwriting, and skill worksheets for seatwork. It was mostly meaningless busy work to my students and a nightmare for grading and record keeping. In all fairness though, I have to say that my students made more progress than I had expected. Setting higher goals increased some students' achievement.

With three years of experience, I began teaching first grade at a suburban public school. During my first year at this school, I taught from a very old basal series, which my team of four first-grade teachers had supplemented with additional reading, writing, and math activities. Our reading time consisted of listening to stories, oral reading, silent reading, partner reading, writing and illustrating class books, journal writing, graphing, discussing stories and experiences, teaching skills, and standardized assessment. This was more like the instruction I had learned about in college. It was a relief to teach as part of a team where everyone developed and helped implement ideas. One teacher wrote reading plans for all the first-grade classrooms every week. This enabled all first-grade children to have common lessons for reading and experience the same activities. My colleagues and I could then talk about the problems we were having and brainstorm ideas as a group. The following year we changed our reading series, and we now have an even more balanced approach, which I will explain later. I am glad to be where I am today, and I am fortunate to have had these experiences. Yet, I still feel the need to add components to my program in order to effectively reach more children and to balance and diversify my classroom.

Balanced Reading

Balanced reading does not mean the same thing to every teacher. Words that become overused in education tend to lose their meaning or become so vague that no one can define them anymore. Balanced reading is an idea that teachers have used for years. It is the process that goes on behind the scenes when all of us decide what and how to teach. Essentially, the balanced reading approach is deciding what is important to the teaching of reading, using various aspects of different approaches. It is somewhat like the eclectic approach, but is more reasoned than just picking and choosing a little of this and a little of that. Let me share with you what I believe is a balanced reading approach for first grade and some of the ways I incorporate it in my classroom. My program includes five things: reading, writing, skills, assessment, and home involvement.

Reading

Reading is done in many different ways in a balanced program. One way is for the teacher, or a student, to read aloud to the whole class. I have story time daily. Another way to read is for the whole class to read the same book aloud together. Sometimes, this is a big book that we all share. Sometimes each student may have his or her own small text, or it may be a basal reader. At other times, students may partner read or read silently. They may read together in groups using copies of the same book, or they may read a book of their choosing. From time to time, one student may read to another student while he or she listens, or a student may read individually to an adult. A strategy found in the *Pegasus Teacher's Implementation Guide* (Shaw & Santa, 1993, p. 36) is wonderful for emergent readers. For this strategy, which focuses on repeated readings of pattern books, we use four sets of books for emergent readers, each set written on a different first-grade reading level. Students have a packet of four sheets that they keep in their desks. These sheets list all of the titles in each level and have spaces on which to write tally marks. Students can choose their own level or they can be assigned. I allow my students to choose a book to begin with from their level. They must read the book to themselves five times, to a partner once, and then to an adult. When the book is read to another person, that person initials the student's sheet. Students keep track of how many times they have read a book, using tally marks. This is a great way to keep track of student reading as well as to provide choice during a free time activity. Reading is done for many reasons: to practice skills, to answer questions, for enjoyment, to understand more about our world, to share with our friends, to relax, to have fun, or to demonstrate our learning. "Children who participate in a Balanced Reading Program are read to [or read] many times in the course of a day" (Depree et al., 1990, p. 5).

Writing

Classroom writing also comes in many forms. Students write in their journals daily. Journals are made from about 25 sheets of writing paper stapled between two pieces of construction paper or the two large parts of a cereal box. Writing assignments may be on a subject of their choice or an assigned topic. Sometimes writing takes the form of class books. This writing may involve completing a given sentence in a student's own words, copying print and adding to it, or writing sentences and stories of their own. Writing sometimes includes experience charts, letters, dictionary entries, Venn diagrams, subject journals, graphing activities, and, yes, even worksheets.

Skills

I believe strongly in skills and direct instruction. Since I realize how important they are to reading, I have been reluctant to take them lightly. We do not have a skill workbook, and I feel that our reading series does not emphasize skills enough. Working as a team, my colleagues and I decide when we will teach each skill. We spend some time directly instructing children, and at other times we teach the skill from a story or poem that we may be reading. For example, in first grade, one of the main tasks is to teach short and long vowel sounds. If I were teaching short "a," I would introduce the sound by saying it and showing pictures of words that contain the sound. I would stress this sound each time I spoke it or came across it during the day. After the initial introduction to short "a," and throughout the time that I was focusing on it, I would directly and indirectly provide opportunities for my students to be exposed to this sound. I would have my students complete worksheets, read and listen to stories and poems, make word lists, play games, write stories, and even eat foods that were related to the short "a" sound. If I felt that a student needed more time on a certain skill, I would perhaps reteach, do worksheets in small groups, or assign additional partner or group activities.

Assessment

At my school, letter grades are not assigned until third grade. Our report cards show "Improvement Needed," "Acceptable Progress," or "Good Progress." Marks are given in oral reading, word analysis, comprehension, and sight vocabulary. It is becoming more difficult to mark these categories, though, as our teaching styles and emphases are changing. We are getting away from round-robin reading and comprehension testing that these marks were based on in the past. Our teaching approaches have changed faster than the assessment forms, and they need to be updated in the near future. Assessment is done in a variety of ways. We use journal writing, where students use inventive spelling, to get clues about their phonic knowledge. Listening to our students read stories and word lists aloud is another form of evaluation. In addition, observation, class discussion, and skills testing are used to analyze our students' progress. I keep a type of portfolio on each student, but I would not say that I use portfolio assessment. I select the work I want to keep, but I eventually send it all home by the end of the year. I believe I struggle the most with assessment.

Home Involvement

Lastly, home involvement is a large part of a balanced reading program. If a child completes reading activities at school, but never sees the importance of reading at home, he or she will begin to believe that reading is not important. Since our reading books are like magazines and would get ruined easily if they traveled home with students, we have devised other ways to encourage reading at home.

Much of the writing that is done in class is put together to form class books. Each book contains a page completed by a different child or group, as well as a place for parental comments. The students check out class books on a nightly basis and read them at home with their parents. Usually, parents write comments that I read aloud to the class the following day. This gets parents involved in reading with their children and sharing in their schoolwork. Students are also encouraged to share their library books, as well as their completed classroom journals with their families. When a journal is finished, it goes home for an evening so each child can show off his or her work. Another way families can share books is with the Pizza Hut "Book It" program. My requirements are that each child read, or have read to him or her, four books a month. The child has to write about and draw a picture of his or her favorite part of each book. Additionally, I have backpacks that go home with students throughout the winter. These backpacks contain games, books, and activities that can be done at home with the student's family. Families get to keep them for one weekend. Another backpack is for our classroom teddy bear, Ardmore. He loves to travel and goes with anyone who is going on a trip. Parents and children must write about Ardmore's trip in his journal, which is read aloud upon his return. (This year Ardmore went to Scotland!)

A major focus of parent involvement in my classroom is for parents to help students learn their theme words. We have eight themes for the year, and each list has approximately twenty words. See the Figure 3.1 for lists of themes and theme words. Parents work with their children daily in learning and reviewing these words. When the words are mastered, a parent signs and returns the form and the student reads the words to me. Memorization is sometimes looked down upon in today's reading

Figure 3.1: Theme Words for Units of Study from Heath Basal

Theme 1: Communication		Theme 2: Family	
a	in	and	is
an	it	bad	mom
at	like	brother	more
black	on	dad	my
blue	red	family	she
brown	school	get	sister
can	to	good	the
green	yellow	grandma	when
I	you	grandpa	with
if	we	he	your

Theme 3: Silly Stuff		Theme 4: Changes	
back	no	are	little
cat	not	baby	moon
come	out	ball	old
did	said	change	same
do	see	cold	saw
dog	silly	day	sun
down	too	egg	then
go	went	fly	this
house	will	frog	up
look	yes	grow	what

Theme 5: Meet the Mammals		Theme 6: Let's Eat	
animals	long	above	lunch
bear	mouse	around	mix
born	play	bake	noodles
eat	size	cheese	people
have	sleep	cook	pizza
help	spring	cookies	ready
his	they	eat	soup
kind	very	favorite	taste
little	water	ground	there
live	winter	know	under
		like	vegetables

Theme 7: Ecology		Theme 8: Friends and Neighbors	
air	need	always	people
birds	place	around	share
care	plants	blew	special
city	pond	community	store
earth	rescue	country	storm
ecology	save	friends	street
fish	snail	job	together
garden	splash	much	town
help	water	neighbor	trash
insects	wild	neighborhood	wind
		parade	zoo

programs, but I believe that it still has its place in learning. Some students do memorize theme words, or even whole stories. This gives them confidence to read aloud and provides a good base of sight words to build on.

What a Balanced Day is Like

In order for you to put this all into perspective, let me explain what a typical day is like in my classroom. The first activity of my students' day is journal writing. At the beginning of the year, students draw in their journals and label their pictures. Sometimes they even copy words they see around the room into their journals. After a few weeks, students begin to write sentences with inventive spelling. By spring break, some students are writing full pages. I usually give my students story starters, or writing ideas, but if they have their own ideas, I never discourage them. I really do not care what they write about as long as they write. About once or twice a week, I do not give any directions for writing. I call this "Free Day," and students can write as they please. Most students really enjoy this freedom. Journal time lasts from 15 to 30 minutes, and we do it every morning. During journal time I may be reading journal pages and writing comments, listening to individuals read theme words, helping a child write a new word in his dictionary, or giving additional assistance in writing and spelling.

After journal time, I have calendar time. One thing that I do during this time is write the daily news. The children tell me what is happening today at school, what is going on with their families, and things that are happening in the world. They dictate to me, I write it, and we read it aloud together. Calendar time is also an opportunity to read the new comments that were written in our class books. I choose a new person to take each book for the evening. If Ardmore Bear has returned from a trip, I read his journal at this time, too. Calendar time takes about 30 minutes.

Next, we move into our reading time, which lasts about 90 minutes. Activities vary from day to day, but we always read a poem aloud from a large chart. We may read the same poem for a whole week. When the students are comfortable with the print, I choose one of them to point to the words as the whole class reads. After our poem, or poems, we spend time reading from a big book. There are two big books for each of our themes, so we read the same book for two weeks. Depending on the day, I may read the book aloud while the students listen, or they may listen to a taped reading or singing of the book. On other days, they may read from their small books while I read from the big book. Students may partner read, read silently, or we may all read the book with or without the tape. When we are finished reading, we do additional activities based on the theme. We may do a graphing activity such as "Which character would you like to be?" or "Would you rather have spaghetti or macaroni?" We may read a similar book and make a comparison chart or a Venn diagram. If the book has a lot of rhyming words, we might list the words that rhyme, put them in alphabetical order, or look for short vowels throughout the story. In other cases, we may make a class book similar to our theme book. If the character in the story went on a journey to the jungle and saw many things, we might pretend we went on a visit to Venus and write about what we saw.

Sometimes during our reading time, we have centers. Some of my centers have included the following: listening station, reading a book of your choice, using the class computer, playing a game which involves a reading skill, using letter stamps, or writing about pictures that were created with stencils. My students also make bingo cards with their theme words. Bingo is played by the whole class, with one or more students calling the words. All students also have their own dictionary in which they write their theme words. Theme words were chosen by the reading manual and include those words that are vital to understanding each theme. These theme words include many basic sight words. Students keep a set of theme flash cards in their desks which they use to play memory, put words in alphabetical order, or just to quiz themselves.

Right after lunch, I begin by reading a story aloud. The only thing I expect from children at this time is that they sit back and enjoy the story; however, it is a very important time of the day and a vital part of a balanced reading program. "In setting aside time to read purely for the sake of reading, you'll show children that doing so is valuable" (Depree et al., 1990, p. 6). The remaining part of my day consists of math, science, and social studies, into which other activities using reading and writing are incorporated, but are not the main focus. If there is any free time during the afternoon, students may have an additional center time, free reading, or time to read books for emergent readers.

All in all, I feel that a balanced reading program does more to reach every student than pigeonholing myself into a single form of reading instruction. Incorporating the best parts of many teaching methods can help us to become more versatile in our approaches and, therefore, better reading teachers. I am sure that it is the goal of every reading teacher to nurture good readers. Just as an athlete takes many steps to become a worthy contender, we should be using many approaches to ensure good readers. If a classroom teacher uses only one format to teach reading, students will not be fully prepared to interpret print. I am not advocating the departure from any approach you may now be using. What I am proposing is that we use what we have while continuing to add to, change, and rearrange our present formats in order to obtain a balanced approach to teaching reading.

Authentic Reading and Writing in a Skills-Based Basal Reading Program

Christine Truckenmiller

The development of the IRA/NCTE Standards for the English Language Arts (1996) was guided by the vision that all students must have the opportunities and resources to develop the language skills they need to pursue life's goals and to participate fully as informed, productive members of society. It is a vision and responsibility that causes me to feel inadequate as an educator. It is this feeling of being inadequate that motivates me to strive to learn about and implement various language arts techniques and methods in my second-grade classroom so that my students will have opportunities and resources available to develop the language skills needed.

I teach reading using a traditional skills-based basal program. This is the reading program that my school currently mandates. In this approach, specific skills are taught and reviewed explicitly. Because this approach to teaching reading can be very limiting, I feel that it is important to also provide opportunities for authentic reading and writing. The dictionary defines the word authentic as genuine. I hope to provide reading and writing activities that are genuine for my students—opportunities in which students are allowed to explore and experiment with language in a way that is enjoyable and meaningful. Research has shown that writing leads to improved reading achievement, reading leads to better writing performance, and combined instruction leads to improvements in both areas (Sweet, 1994).

I have chosen several strategies to use with my class to increase the opportunities available for authentic reading and writing. I have adapted the strategies in ways that allow me to use them in my classroom situation, where a basal series is still the primary means of reading instruction.

Reader's Workshop

Reader's workshop is an organizational scheme providing for the full integration of children's literature into the classroom (Reutzel & Cooter, 1992; Swift, 1993). This approach is typically not designed for classrooms where reading is taught using the traditional basal approach, so I have had to modify the idea to fit my situation. I have designed a version of reader's workshop which will work within the framework of my classroom and will still integrate children's literature into each school day. I want the students to be free to choose and respond to literature in an enjoyable way.

Reader's Workshop as a Center

I plan to create a reader's workshop center in my classroom. This center will be used daily during my reading instruction time. Students who are not reading a selection from the basal or working on skills with me will be able to work independently at the reader's workshop center. The center will be a designated area in the room that will contain tubs of books, suggestions for responding to literature, and the materials needed to do so.

Selecting and Responding to Literature

During reader's workshop, the students will self-select books from tubs containing various genres. After reading the selection alone or with a study buddy, a plan for responding to and sharing the book will be designed. Because my plan for reader's workshop calls for independent study, a flow chart will be posted in the center so students can follow the sequence of steps. These basic steps will be followed by the students:

1. Choose a book to read.
2. Log in—write the date and title of the selection in the log.
3. Read the selection at least once.
4. Log out—write the date finished, number of pages read, and the plan to respond to and share the book.
5. Prepare for sharing.
6. Share the selection with a peer, small group, or whole class.

A variety of literature-response activities will be suggested and modeled before the students begin working independently. These activities for responding to a book will be introduced and modeled during a focus lesson one day each week. The early focus lessons will include lots of modeling, including teaching the students to choose appropriate books to read. The students will be encouraged to choose books that look interesting and have few unknown words. If a student is really interested in a book that is too difficult for him or her, that book could be put on tape or it could be read with a study buddy. I will encourage the students to choose a variety of books to read and respond to. I will also model how to follow the flow chart. Future focus lessons will be used to introduce the various methods of sharing literature, as well as new concepts such as genre and author studies. Also, students' needs will guide plans for future focus lessons. Listed in Figure 3.2 are a number of literature response activities that reinforce many areas of the language arts.

After choosing one of the activities listed or creating an original plan, the student will decide with whom to share the story. If the student wants to share with a peer or a small group, this will happen during the allotted reading period. Students who wish to share their stories and response with the entire class will do so at the daily story time.

Reader's Workshop Materials

In the center I would like to have some control of the books from which the students can choose. I will have several tubs with books from different genres, such as poetry, fiction, nonfiction, and biography. Within each genre, I will need to provide books at various ability levels. I would also like to include several of the books in each genre on tape. This tape could be recorded each week by a classroom volunteer.

Students will also keep a log of books read. This log will be kept at the center. Each time students begin a new book, the date and title will be noted. When students finish the book, the date, the number of pages read, and their plan for responding to that particular book will be noted in the log. This log can be used to monitor the students' progress, and it allows students to monitor their own progress as plans are made for future selections. Also, a sense of accomplishment and pride may be fostered by looking back at the number of books read and shared over the course of the year.

Within the center, the student will also be able to locate literature response suggestion sheets or posters. The basic materials needed to respond should also be found within the center if the student is going to be encouraged to be creative and work independently. A dry erase board will be available in the center so that students can list other materials that are needed in the center.

Figure 3.2: Literature Response Activities

Book Cover:	Create a new book cover for the story. Explain it.
Radio Advertisement:	Write and tape-record a radio advertisement that will make other students want to read the story.
Map:	Make a map of the area where the story took place. Indicate where each event occurred and include a key.
Puppet Show:	Create puppets and perform a puppet show of the story.
Play:	Write and perform a play about the story.
Read/Record:	Tape-record the story in your best reading voice, complete with sound effects.
Diary:	Write a diary for one of your characters telling what happened to him or her.
T.V. Commercial:	Write and perform a TV commercial to sell the book.
Book Recommendation:	Write your recommendations in a letter to a friend or make a sign that can attach to a door knob, and deliver your door hanger to another classroom door.
Character Sketch:	Sketch a portrait of a character and write or tell everything about him or her.
New Ending:	Create a new ending for the story. Explain how and why you changed the original ending.
Poem:	Write and illustrate a poem about the story.
Drawings:	Make a series of five drawings depicting the major points of the story.
Flannel Board Story:	Create and retell the story.
Read to a Friend:	Read your book to a friend.
Display:	Make a display of items mentioned in the book. Explain their significance.
Demonstration:	Demonstrate how to make or do something learned from the story
Letter to Author:	Write a letter to the author giving your reaction to the book.
Story Chain:	Summarize a chapter or story, sequence story events, or review story elements.

A Quality Classroom Library

Another opportunity for authentic reading in my classroom can be offered by establishing a classroom library. However, just having books available in my classroom is not enough. My goal is to provide a well designed library to entice students to read throughout the school day.

Morrow (1985), Morrow and Weinstein (1982), and Routman (1991) identify a number of physical features of classroom libraries that increase children's voluntary use of books:

- Focal area that is named: The area is attractive and highly visible. A name indicates that the library is an important part of the classroom.

- Partitioned and private: Boundaries set apart the library from the classroom and afford a quiet place to read.

- Comfortable seating: Without seating, students may be less likely to use the library. Seating may include carpet, chairs, beanbags, or pillows.

- Five to eight books per student: Various books can be read and discussed by students.

- Books that provide a variety of genres and reading levels: This variety may include picture storybooks, informational books, poetry, and chapter books.

- Organized into categories: Books can be organized by genre, theme, topic, author, reading level, content area, or some combination of these features.

- Room for at least five students: Sufficient space promotes the building of a community of readers who enjoy and discuss literature.

- Two types of shelving: Open shelves entice the reader by displaying attractive covers. Shelves with books displayed spine out offer the capability of providing more books using minimal space.

- Literature-oriented displays and props: Primary-grade students enjoy flannel boards, books on tape, stuffed animals, and puppets.

Silent Reading and Read-Aloud Times

As educators, we know that our students need to spend time reading and being exposed to quality literature. Two simple ways of providing for this, even in a traditional basal approach classroom, are to allow daily time for silent reading and to read aloud to our students.

DEAR is an acronym for Drop Everything And Read. This is a special time each day when we put away all of our other studies and take time to read and enjoy books. Reading silently establishes reading as a lifelong habit. It also makes students better readers because they get better at whatever they practice. I provide practice time each day for approximately fifteen minutes. During DEAR time, the students read books from home, the classroom library, or the school library. The students are free to sit with their friends in any area of the classroom. I also read silently during this time. Bernice E. Cullinan (1992) offers several benefits of silent reading. She notes that silent reading expands a child's world, develops independence as a learner, stirs the imagination, establishes a reading habit, develops vocabulary, increases fluency, and develops understanding of other people.

A favorite time in my classroom is story time. This is a time when I read to the students, and the students read aloud stories which they have published. I vary the books I read from simple picture books to chapter books. I try to highlight the author and illustrator of each book. We usually begin each session by reading the title and predicting what the book will be about. We briefly discuss the book after reading it. We might discuss the author's purpose for writing the book, new vocabulary, or the medium used by the illustrator to create the artwork. Story time is an excellent opportunity for me to express my excitement and love for books to the students. It's neat to see that the books I read aloud at story time are the same ones that many students seek and read during DEAR time and when they go to the library. Reading aloud to students opens doors to worlds unknown, gives them an educational advantage, and makes written language easier for them to understand as they read alone (Cullinan, 1992).

Writer's Workshop

Classroom teachers as well as writing researchers have discovered that even young children want to communicate through writing, and they can begin writing as they are learning to read or even before they read (Bissex, 1980; Chomsky, 1971; Graves, 1983).

Writer's workshop is typically an established daily period of time in which students write and publish stories on topics of their choosing. Students work through the stages of the writing process at their own pace (Tompkins, 1994). Skill-based basal programs generally do not emphasize the writing component of language arts. I feel strongly that my students need to be given opportunities to incorporate the skills taught during reading class into authentic writing. I feel it is important that the students' writing not always be teacher or text directed, but part of a creative process.

Because of my classroom situation, I've adapted the writer's workshop approach detailed in *Teaching Writing: Balancing Process and Product* (Tompkins, 1994). Writer's workshop is designed as a center in my classroom, but the goal is still to allow students to create stories on topics of their choice. Instead of the typical daily focus lesson, I provide one focus lesson each week and the students work independently at the center for the remainder of the week. The beginning focus lessons are designed to teach the writing process. Through modeling and guided activities, the students are involved in pre-writing, rough draft writing, peer conferencing, editing, teacher conferencing, publishing, and sharing. Early in the year, we learn to create stories using the story elements as a guide. Creating different types of books is also taught. Other focus lessons are based on the needs of the students as they arise.

I've offered writer's workshop in this form for two years in my classroom. I've been pleased with the students' excitement for writing and the growth that they have displayed. Writing is a very individual process, and the growth each student makes varies greatly, but I've seen improvement in writing skills from my struggling, average, and gifted students. Just as importantly, I've seen students gain confidence in themselves as writers and communicators.

Materials

I provide a variety of tools for the writers in my classroom. The center contains many different types of paper for rough drafts and publishing: crayons, markers, colored pencils, stapler, paper clips, book rings, yarn, paper fasteners, construction paper, poster board, wallpaper, a junior thesaurus, a dictionary, and directions for making different kinds of books. A flow chart is also posted so that the students are always clear on the major steps involved in the writing process.

Wee Deliver In-School Postal Service

The in-school postal service is part of the U.S. Postal Service's campaign to "Stamp Out Illiteracy." The U.S. Postal Service will send a free informational video and start-up kit to any school that requests a kit (U.S. Postal Service, 1991). The objectives of the program include:

1. To provide students with real-life experience in which to apply basic skills: addressing envelopes using the mail system, and writing a letter using punctuation appropriate for letters.
2. To unify the entire student body through a student-centered, school-wide communication system.
3. To provide a vehicle for students to use the writing skills learned through the process of writing strategies.
4. To improve language arts skills.

I have only used this program for one year, and I used it just within my classroom, not school wide. I also did not assign specific jobs such as postmaster, sorter, etc. The daily helpers took care of all of the checking of letters, sorting, and delivering.

We needed to create addresses to begin the postal program. Our class decided that we would live in Puppy, IL. The students lived on six different "streets," including Bulldog Blvd., Collie Rd., and Dalmation Dr. Students then created their own home addresses such as 1368 W. Dalmation Dr., Puppy, IL 61032. We compiled all of our complete addresses into an address book that students kept in their desks. Focus lessons centered around writing parts of friendly letters and addressing envelopes.

The mini post office in the classroom contained a mailbox, stamps, envelopes, sorter, and carrier mail bag. A giant letter and envelope were posted nearby so that the students could refer to them and see if their letters contained the five parts of a friendly letter, and also so they could check the placement of addresses on envelopes. The Postal Service Teacher's Guide contains instructions for implementing the entire program.

Students are encouraged to write a letter to a peer whenever they may have a free moment. I established several guidelines for letter writing: nothing can be written that would make another person feel bad, and if you receive a letter you must write back. These guidelines were established just to be sure that the program remained a positive one. The program is a great way to encourage authentic writing. Students love to receive letters so they are motivated to write letters. This year I want to expand my program to include the third-graders.

Conclusion

My professional goal is to continue to strive toward providing my students with the opportunities and resources to develop the language skills they need to pursue their goals and to participate fully as informed, productive members of society who have a love for reading and writing. I believe this can be accomplished by providing balanced instruction in language arts. Balanced instruction combines the best elements from phonics instruction and the whole language approach as well as other approaches. Diegmueller (1996b) states that a balanced approach is occurring when students are explicitly taught the relationship between letters and sounds in a systematic fashion, and they are being read to and are reading interesting stories and writing at the same time. As a professional, I need to continue to strive to translate my goal of providing balanced reading instruction into practice.

Maintaining Balance in a First-Grade Classroom

Linda Mast

As an undergraduate student and as a preservice teacher during the beginning of the 1990's, I was bombarded with anti-phonics, anti-basal theory and filled with the notion that teaching all students to read using whole language was the best approach. Using basal readers, workbook pages, focusing on phonics skills, and having reading groups (ways I was taught to read in the 1970's) were being labeled as taboo. I began my career excitedly with ambitions of using real books, language experience, and engaging in purposeful and meaningful reading and writing with my students.

Regardless of how excellent a college's undergraduate teacher education program is, or how successful a student teaching experience is, we know that important knowledge and experience are gained within our own classrooms. As a first year, first-grade teacher, I was told my students would have to progress through three pre-primer books, a primer, and a first reader before the end of May, which was when the district's local assessments were to be given. The students were all at different developmental levels of literacy. They needed phonics instruction. They needed to be taught certain skills. They needed to learn how to read and write, and they needed to get through five required books. I was extremely grateful for the teacher's manual and clung to it desperately. Although feeling guilty about betraying my undergraduate studies, I taught phonics, used basal readers, and yes, assigned workbook pages. To ensure I was not doing a horrible injustice to my students, I tried to supplement the basal program with trade books relating to themes within the social studies and science curriculum. Some things worked and some things did not. To my surprise and delight, students progressed through the five readers, passed the district assessment, and, most importantly, they were reading and writing.

During subsequent years, while alternating teaching assignments between first and second grade, as well as teaching a split classroom one year, my grip on the manual loosened a bit, yet the foundation for my reading instruction continued to be the district's basal reading series. As I became more familiar with first-grade skills, vocabulary, and development, I used more trade books in an attempt to integrate the curriculum with quality literature; nevertheless, I was never confident that I was doing the right thing. The beginning of my graduate work in the area of reading and the many workshops I attended on various reading topics (whole language, literature-based instruction, integrated curriculum, and content area reading) always left me feeling as if I needed to be either more whole language or more phonics oriented. Questions from other teachers or parents such as "Are you whole language?" or "Do you use the phonics approach?" made me very uncomfortable. It was not until recently that I realized I will never fit solidly beneath either of those labels, and I am not sure that any teacher should.

Currently there are many different labels for approaches to reading instruction: basal readers, whole language, literature based, language experience, and phonics. All approaches have their strengths as well as weaknesses; therefore, there can be no one right way. Educators must consider and try to balance the good from each approach around the common goal of teaching children to read. With the diverse learners present in classrooms today, aspects from various approaches can benefit students during their journey toward literacy. According to Regie Routman (1991), "The question is no longer *if* phonics should be taught but rather *how* phonics should be taught meaningfully" (p. 147). A balanced approach, where phonics and skills are taught through meaningful and enjoyable literature, may be a very effective way to meet the needs of every learner.

Pat Cunningham identified four key elements which comprise balanced reading instruction: guided reading, self-selected reading, writing, and working with words (Berglund, 1996). These four elements provide the framework for organizing a classroom around balanced literacy development. The following sections describe characteristics of the four elements of a balanced reading program as they apply to my first-grade classroom.

Guided Reading

Beginning readers need to move systematically through text. This is where basal programs can help teachers, especially novice teachers, to introduce grade-appropriate vocabulary and skills, along with reading stories appropriate for beginning readers. Also, using other materials besides basals is important in providing balanced instruction. Teachers familiar with the vocabulary and skills taught to first-grade students can easily find other appropriate text to use, either in conjunction with, or instead of, the basal.

In first grade, much instruction and many activities are directed by and done with the teacher as a whole class. Traditionally, reading instruction has been provided to students in three ability groups: high, average, and low. The whole language movement, on the other hand, encouraged whole group instruction and discouraged ability grouping. The diverse range of ability in first grade means that not everyone in the whole group will be at the same level of instruction and, therefore, all students cannot be expected to be involved in the same activities at all times. If a teacher is to meet the individual needs of his or her students in first grade, where some students have developed sight vocabularies and others have not yet developed the skill of one-to-one matching of spoken word to printed word, ability groups are indeed necessary.

In a balanced reading environment, reading groups are a necessary part of literacy instruction. The difference between grouping in a balanced program and traditional ability grouping is flexibility. Grouping may be done heterogeneously, by ability, or by interest. Grouping really should depend on the needs of the students in a particular classroom and need not stay the same. Not only does flexible grouping allow for individual student needs to be met, but it also allows students to learn from each other and prevents group labels such as the "eagles," "robins," and "buzzards" from affecting student progress and confidence.

Whatever the text, trade book, big book, poem, or song, guided reading in first grade begins with the teacher activating the students' prior knowledge before reading with questions, discussion, or an activity. Next, the story is read aloud to the students while they follow along. There are almost always students already reading who can help out with a page or two, but most of the initial reading should be done by the teacher. This way students can understand and enjoy the text. Predictable pattern books or books containing repetition of certain words and phrases allow all students to join in with the initial reading. The reading is discussed and responded to in open-ended ways, and vocabulary and concepts are related to the children's lives or to other familiar stories.

After being guided through the new text by the teacher, a second reading occurs to allow more student participation. Then the class can be divided into carefully organized, smaller groups to develop specific skills or strategies needed by different learners. While the teacher meets with a small group, the other students can participate in activities involving extension of the story, repeated readings, or vocabulary practice (perhaps in the context of carefully selected workbook pages). Multiple copies of any text used during guided reading should be available for students to select during independent reading time throughout the year.

Self-Selection

In a balanced program, children need to be given the opportunity to choose their own materials for reading and writing. Mary Jo Fresch (1995) observed certain patterns among first-grade students when given opportunities to select reading materials. Fresch noted that children frequently choose books that were familiar to them. Students often select those books to be read aloud by the teacher to the whole class (including big books available in small versions), books read to the children by an adult such as the teacher, librarian, or parent, or the students' own personal favorites. Fresch feels this repetition of familiar material helps children gain control of reading strategies by drawing on what they already know.

Another pattern Fresch (1995) noticed was that students become more confident after spending time with a familiar text. The students she observed had the tendency to select a new unfamiliar book after spending time with a familiar one. This gives students the opportunity, during self-selection time, to apply strategies that they have learned to unfamiliar text. After these attempts, Fresch noticed the students would often return to the security of a known text. Fresch argues that this movement between easy and more difficult text suggests that students also take risks while building confidence if given the opportunity to select their own books.

In my classroom, time for silent, self-selected reading is provided daily. Several times a week, students are given the opportunity to share a story of their choice with a reading buddy.

Also, after completing independent assignments, students are given the choice to either read or write quietly. An important aspect of silent, independent reading of a book is modeling. As the teacher, I model silent reading and buddy reading for my students.

Self-selection during literacy development cannot occur in the classroom without a classroom library. Fractor, Woodruff, Martinez, and Teale (1993) cite research that very few primary students choose to look at books during their free choice time. The authors went on to "identify classroom characteristics that nurture voluntary reading" (p. 477). Some characteristics are: specifying an allotted time for self-selection, providing a variety of genres and reading levels, establishing attractive, accessible library centers (where books are organized into categories), and offering at least five to six books per child. See Figure 3.3 for book selection guide.

Figure 3.3: Book Selection Guide for a Classroom Library

1. Choose high quality children's literature: good authors and good illustrators hold children's attention.
2. Choose a variety of books: fiction, poetry, and information books. Don't forget books without words, alphabet books, and pattern books.
3. Include multicultural literature so that students have opportunities to see their own and other ethnic communities represented in books.
4. Provide books with a range of difficulty so that all students have something to read and also are appropriately challenged.
5. Try to provide at least five to six books per child. Many public libraries offer "book bag" services which provide a multitude of books to be checked out to a classroom teacher for about a month. Books are expensive and this is a great way for a new teacher to provide quality literature in a classroom library while building his or her own collection.
6. Include books about different holidays or topics your class will be studying. Do an attitude and interest inventory with your students early in the school year to find out what kinds of books they like.

After reading about classroom libraries, I began to display as many book covers as possible, rather than just showing the spines on a shelf. Using labeled plastic baskets that display book covers better, I organized books by genre and author, and also by setting up special baskets for "boys' favorites," "girls' favorites," and "teacher favorites." There is also a special table for class books made by the students. As a result, valuable discussion occurs among the children as to which books belong in which baskets when it is clean-up time. A listening center with audio-cassette books and a poetry corner where poetry books and posters are displayed are extensions of the classroom library, where students may choose to interact with literature. With these changes to my classroom library, students are choosing to read more during free time and are finding a greater variety of books to choose from during silent reading or buddy reading. See classroom map in Figure 3.4.

Figure 3.4: Classroom Map

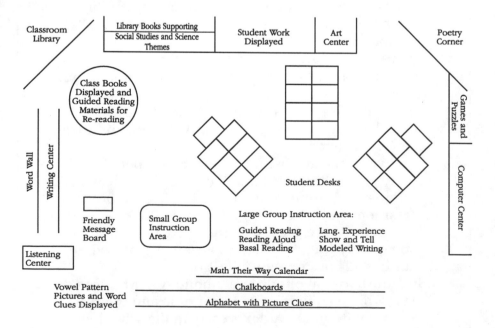

Writing

Like reading, writing instruction must provide a balance between teacher-directed and student-selected activities. Process writing, even at the first-grade level, is extremely beneficial to young writers. In my district, the goal of first-grade writing is not only to write complete sentences, but also to construct a paragraph around a main idea by the end of the year. First-grade students are taught to include a focus sentence, as well as a closing sentence in their paragraph. Just as at any grade level, the more pre-writing activities, the better the writing. In first grade, pre-writing activities usually involve a story or an experience, followed by making a list or creating a web to organize ideas.

Regie Routman (1991) identifies several approaches to use within a balanced writing program. Writing aloud, shared writing, guided writing, and independent writing need to make up a daily writing program.

Writing Aloud

Particularly in first grade, modeling the writing process, or writing aloud, is extremely important. Enabling young children to witness the thought process that goes into writing (thinking, spacing, handwriting, spelling, punctuation, and grammar) gives young students direction in their own writing, as well as providing an excellent opportunity for phonics instruction.

Weekly journal writing occurs in my classroom. At the beginning of the year, children's entries are very structured and are usually a response to a particular activity, story, or poem. For example, when studying plants, I read aloud a story about different kinds of seeds. The class then examines actual seeds during a seed sorting and graphing activity. Afterwards, the class brainstorms a list of descriptive words for seeds and I write the words on chart paper. The journal assignment is then to write sentences telling about seeds. I model sentences such as: "Seeds can be small." "Seeds can be black." While writing these sentences, I point out how each sentence begins with a capital letter, stress spacing between words, and then mention the punctuation at the end of the sentences. The students then use the list of descriptive words and the sentences modeled for them to construct their own sentences in their journals.

Later in the year, on Monday mornings, the students will write in their journals about things that happened over the weekend. I always begin journal time by composing my own entry on the chalkboard in front of the children. They see and hear me sound out words, construct sentences, and apply grammar and punctuation rules while I write. There is usually a specific skill I instruct the children to practice in their journal entry, and I model the skill in my writing. For example, I may include names of the days of the week or include sequence words. I then instruct the students to use those kinds of words in their journal entries.

Shared Writing

Shared writing is when the teacher and students compose together. The teacher does the actual writing, but the choices of words are discussed and agreed upon by the students and teacher. Shared writing has occurred in my classroom in the form of class newsletters, narratives telling about a special event or field trip, class thank you letters to parents and volunteers, and class pen pal letters. Another example of shared writing is constructing a chart with students, by writing down what they know and questions they have about a certain topic, in science or social studies. I like to make individual copies of shared writing compositions for the students in the form of small books. This allows opportunity for re-reading and illustrating. Also, I keep the chart paper containing the original shared writing on display in the classroom, and the children often refer to those stories for help with spelling when doing their own independent writing.

Guided Writing

Guided writing is similar to guided reading, in the sense that the teacher guides students by responding to them and extending their thinking during the process of writing. Assignments for guided writing occur after students have had many opportunities to see writing demonstrated by the teacher. During guided writing, the student does the writing and meets with the teacher for support and suggestions to strengthen the text. Writing mechanics and skills are taught and revisions are made as the need arises in the context of each child's writing. This can be accomplished in whole group settings, small groups, or individually. In first grade, guided writing topics generally stem from science and social studies themes or as a response to literature.

Literature response writings are often put together in the form of class books, which remain on display in my classroom and are available for student checkout. One example of a class book my students created was an extension of a guided reading lesson of *Chicken Soup with Rice* (Sendak, 1990). After a second reading of the story, the class brainstormed a list of action words involved with eating (sipping, chewing, slurping, munching, etc.). Then students came up with a list of food pairs, or foods that go together, like chicken soup with rice (peanut butter and jelly, spaghetti and meatballs, macaroni and cheese, etc.). Using their chosen action word and food pair, students then wrote and illustrated their own page for our book, following the repeated pattern in Sendak's book: "Sipping once, sipping twice, sipping chicken soup with rice."

Independent Writing

According to Routman (1991), the purpose of independent writing "is to build fluency, establish the writing habit, make personal connections, explore meaning, promote critical thinking, and use writing as a natural, pleasurable, self-chosen activity" (p. 67). As mentioned earlier, I often give my students the choice to either read or write after completing assignments throughout the day. Like the importance of allowing time for self-selected reading, students need time to write about self-selected topics and write to self-selected audiences.

Much like the appealing, designated, reading center, my first-grade classroom has a specified writing center where children go to obtain various writing materials and ideas for writing. The writing center contains different kinds of writing paper, drawing paper, envelopes, pencils, markers, crayons, and erasers. I provide cards listing topics for writing, questions, or story starters in small baskets. Frequently, I will display interesting pictures from magazines, science collections, or experiments at the center to encourage students to write about what they see.

Next to the writing center is what I call a Friendly Message Board, an idea I picked up from a workshop I attended. It is actually an old painting easel with pockets attached to it. The pockets used inside library books work very well. There is a pocket labeled for each person in the class, including the teacher. This is where students can leave notes for me or a friend. I initiate the activity by writing to every child on the first day of school, welcoming them to my classroom. I encourage children to write back and let them know there will be free time to write to a friend. Each day I try to write a short note to three different children in my class to keep the Friendly Message Board alive. After a lesson on the parts of a friendly letter and after reading a basal story called *The Surprise Letters* (Wiseman, 1989), the class writes mystery letters to each other, leaving clues as to who the writer is.

Working With Words (Phonics)

The final component of a balanced reading program is phonics instruction. One problem with teaching phonics in isolation is that most young children have no idea how the sounds they are connecting with letters relate to reading. Freppon and Dahl (1991) stress an important principle of phonics instruction. They feel that "phonics instruction should begin when children exhibit knowledge of some foundation ideas about written language" (p. 196). Children must first have some understanding that written language has meaning and purpose. Freppon and Dahl go on to state that "children lacking these foundation concepts of meaningfulness cannot benefit from instruction about abstract sound-symbol relations" (p. 196).

Beginning reading instruction has sometimes been equated with teaching phonics systematically and sequentially in isolation. Routman (1991) states that reading involves the use of all three cueing systems interdependently: semantic, syntactic, and graphophonic. Routman believes that graphophonic, or letter-sound cues, are the least important of the cueing systems for reading comprehension to occur. In other words, proficiency in phonics alone cannot elicit comprehension. This is demonstrated by students who are able to "sound out" an entire sentence, phoneme by phoneme, and have no clue as to what they just read.

Church (1994) also raises an important question about children who cannot make sense of classroom reading and writing experiences involved with whole language because of underlying difficulties with language. Children who do not seem to be progressing as readers and writers in a whole language classroom are often referred to reading resource teachers or speech and language therapists for help. Church reports that many of these children simply need more explicit phonics instruction and information about how language works in order to progress as readers. I have encountered children who have been developmentally behind in their expressive and receptive language abilities. These students do not just pick up sounds or a sight vocabulary without explicit instruction because they are still struggling with speaking and understanding complete sentences.

Trachtenburg (1990) describes "an approach that combines the two (phonics and whole language) in a complementary manner—a method that presents the two as mutually supportive and taught in a manner that makes the interrelationships clear to children" (p. 648). Wray (1989) argues that readers should be taught to apply both phonic knowledge and an understanding of context to the task of reading. Such a balanced approach can be attained by providing phonics instruction within the context of literature.

Trachtenburg (1990) suggests a "whole-part-whole" sequence for integrating phonics instruction with children's literature. Trachtenburg's procedure is as follows:

1. Whole: Read, comprehend, and enjoy a whole, quality literature selection.
2. Part: Provide instruction in a high utility phonic element by drawing from or extending the preceding text.
3. Whole: Apply the new phonic skill when reading (and enjoying) another whole, high quality, literature selection.

Instruction of a phonic element within a piece of literature with which students are already familiar will better make the connection between sounds, letters, words, and reading. Routman (1991) states that rather than telling students what sounds and letters she is teaching, she has the children discover the sounds and rules from within the literature to engage students in understanding letter/sound associations. This inquiry approach can be implemented through the use of questions such as, "What do you notice about . . .?" or "Can you find any other words with the same sound as . . .?"

Trachtenburg's approach has worked well in my classroom with big books, various trade books, and poems. Besides being "word detectives" and searching familiar stories for words containing certain consonants, blends, or vowel sounds, my students reexamine literature to locate examples of compound words, contractions, homophones, and different parts of speech. Class lists of these different kinds of words are kept on display year round as spelling references. Pat Cunningham's "Word Wall" is another idea which allows for high frequency words from literature to be displayed alphabetically in the classroom for student practice and reference (Berglund, 1996).

It has been suggested that "invented spelling and decoding are mirror-like processes that make use of the same store of phonological knowledge" (Cunningham & Cunningham, 1992, p. 106). Much phonics instruction in first grade occurs in the context of writing instruction. During writing aloud, I sound out words as I write them. When involved in guided writing, I ask students "What sounds do you hear in the word you are trying to write?" Along with the alphabet, vowel picture clues are displayed in the front of the classroom for students to refer to when writing. For the short vowel sounds, pictures of an alligator, elephant, iguana, octopus, and umbrella may be used. For long vowels, pictures of an ape, eel, ice cream, ocean, and unicorn work well. Referring to these picture/word clues helps students sound out words.

A teacher-guided, invented spelling strategy that I am eager to implement into my balanced program was also pioneered by Cunningham and Cunningham (1992). "Making Words" is a 15 minute, daily instructional activity where students are given letters that they manipulate to make words. This activity is a hands-on activity which allows students to discover sound-letter relationships and how to look for patterns in words, both of which are keys to successful decoding. "Making Words" is a whole group activity that requires every student to respond, and it provides important practice for slower learners as well as challenges for advanced students.

Conclusion

If educators, both novice and experienced, are to meet the needs of the variety of learners in today's classrooms, they cannot rely on only one method of reading instruction. Children have different needs, they learn in different ways, and they progress at different rates. Teachers need to teach using different strategies, flexible grouping, and techniques that they as professionals feel will best serve their students. Providing a balanced approach, within the framework of guided reading, self-selected reading, writing, and phonics instruction, can put an end to the "great debate" over phonics vs. whole language and direct the focus toward effective literacy instruction.

Components of an Ever-Changing Language Arts Program

Dawn Hinz

When I was in college (1990–1994), I rarely heard the word "phonics" so I was pretty much left to figure it out on my own. Through college, "whole language" was the buzz word on campus. Each teacher that I came in contact with had a different definition for the term whole language. I found that preparing for an interview was going to be tougher than I thought. Not only did I have to come up with a definition of phonics, I also had to learn about ten different meanings of whole language! Surprisingly, I managed to make it through all my interviews without a single mention of either of them.

My first year of teaching involved a basal series, and I was very content with that type of teaching. I was told which skills to teach at what times. I was given complete instructions on how to teach reading. The following year, my district adopted a new series, one that used real literature. I wondered how I was going to teach children how to read. The vocabulary didn't build like a basal, and the skills were scattered all over the place. Over the course of the year, teaching reading had some ups and downs. I made many changes and I know many changes are yet to come. There are typically four parts to my language arts program: warm-up, reading, writing, and word and vocabulary study.

Warm-Up

During a warm-up exercise I might choose a poem or a song. This activity engages the entire class in language and rhythm. At this time, I also include some phonics. If we are working on long "a," we may go through a poem and underline all the long "a" words. I have found that many students find this activity illuminating. Students who hadn't picked up on a particular skill during our focus lesson would see it in a different light and grasp hold of it. I would never skip the warm-up activity. Whether I'm introducing something new or reviewing, I have found these activities to be very valuable.

Reading

The first thing I do is reread a familiar text/big book orally. Many times, if I am reading a familiar text, I will retype a portion of it leaving out every fifth word. This is a modified cloze activity; the difference is that they've seen the text before. Using the overhead projector, I call on students to tell me all the possible words that make sense. After a list is generated, I fill in the first letter of the word. Sometimes I have to add a second and third letter, because more than one answer could fit. Many times I will leave part of the word in the blank from the start. For example, "The *icken* crossed the road." I do this to reinforce blends and digraphs. If I choose a big book, I may cover entire words or parts of words with "sticky notes" (you need two "sticky notes" because students can see through only one). I only cover one word on each page and sometimes every few pages, depending on the length of the book. Together we generate possible responses. I uncover the first letter and sometimes more until we all agree on the word.

The next section of reading is devoted to a focus-lesson (sometimes called a minilesson). There are numerous lessons that can be taught: directionality, vocabulary, fluency/phrasing, letters and sounds, spelling patterns, word structure, voice-print matching, and many more.

Another component of my reading program is oral reading practice. I use an anthology, trade book, big book, or even a poem. We might use choral reading, echo reading, shared reading, or guided reading.

I also provide additional oral reading practice using materials that are at each student's instructional level. At this time, students are grouped in a number of different ways. Some are reading independently, some are in a group of two to three students, and some are with me. Typically the group that I am with has about five students. This group usually has the same three students who are having the toughest time in reading. The other two members are chosen at random. The two that get to join the group feel privileged to be there. Somehow, by grouping in this way, I've found that no one looks down upon this group as "dumb"—rather just "lucky." Johnny said to me one day, "We are so lucky! We get to be in your group a lot."

Another aspect of reading is where students respond to reading. We may dramatize parts of a story, do a writing response, or do an art response with writing.

After Lunch Sign-Up

I have a piece of paper in my room where a student can sign up to read a book to the class. I had 100 percent participation in my class last year. The sign-up sheet has a space for the book title and student name. After lunch we have a ten to 15 minute time frame where two students read a book of their choice to the class. This has the most amazing benefit. In order to read, students have to practice this book for their "big day." I put a lot of emphasis on practicing the book they have chosen. Very popular titles are only allowed to be read to the class three times; then they are retired from the sign-up sheet. I don't discourage students from reading those books on their own, but I have noticed that their attention spans run out at about the third time. Another concern may be the length of the book. Students have about five minutes, and they are fully aware of this time frame. When their time is up, I simply say, "Thank you for sharing this book with us. And if anyone wants to find out more about this book, you can find it in our library. Let's put our hands together for _____." Most students finish within five to seven minutes. Students love this time. When a new sign-up sheet goes up, they can hardly wait to put their names on it.

Writer's Workshop

Just as reading started out with a focus-lesson, so does writing. Many of the focus-lessons in reading overlap with the writing, and they include: assisted spelling, sound segmentation, spelling patterns, conventions (spacing, forms, etc.), phonemic awareness activities, blending, endings, and specific letters and sounds. At the conclusion of this session, we create a sentence together, cut it up, and resequence it. It's quick and easy but very beneficial for those struggling readers.

During writer's workshop, the first ten minutes are completely quiet. The timer is set and everybody understands that this is a quiet time so that each person can think and get their beginning thoughts down on paper. When the timer goes off, they are allowed to get up and sit anywhere in the room, as long as they make a "good choice." All students know that a "good choice" is a place where they won't be tempted to get off-task. This time lasts for ten minutes also. For the last five minutes, students can finish their journals, read what they wrote to a friend, or find a book. While all of this is going on, I conference with students, usually five a day.

Conferencing is hard to describe. It is so different with each child. A conference can last a few seconds to a few minutes. I also have a parent in the room at this time. A different parent is signed up for each day of the week. At the beginning of the year, I had parents sign up to be in my class on certain days at specific times. Parents help with publishing pieces of finished writing. Once the writing is published, the author illustrates it and reads it to the class. The piece of work is then added to our class library.

Word and Vocabulary Study

This area of reading usually consists of three parts: word walls, word families, and making words (Cunningham & Hall, 1994a, 1994b). During a word wall activity, I will usually add three words at a time. We put the three words in sentences and discuss the beginning, middle, and end of each of the three words. On a particular day that I am not adding a word to the word wall, we review words already on the wall. During a word family activity, we brainstorm words that have the same vowel and consonant ending and put them in a house together. For example, the letters "at" can make the words rat, sat, mat, cat, hat, etc. After brainstorming words, I put them in a house so now they are a family. I take a piece of tag board and cut it into four parts, and I place a construction paper roof on each house. Another great advantage to these houses is that the word wall does not get overloaded. See Figure 3.5.

Figure 3.5

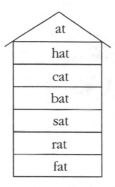

Conclusion

These are all the major components of my language arts program. I am not able to fit in all these components every day, but I try to balance the activities. I know that each year my program will change, but I feel confident that I am working toward a balanced reading program.

Creating a Balanced
Reading Program in First Grade

Rhonda L. Waggoner

Over the years phonics, basal readers, language experience, and literature based instruction have all been used to teach children to read. Each approach or strategy has its own strengths that affect each child's reading success. In the quest to create a balanced reading program, I have tried to use a combination of these approaches to help meet individual differences of children in a diverse, heterogeneous first-grade classroom (Cunningham & Allington, 1994). In this article, I will discuss the organization and instruction that create the balanced reading program in my first-grade classroom.

Classroom Organization

My classroom is arranged to have different places for children to meet in large and small groups (see Figure 3.6). Desks are arranged in two semicircles to foster discussion between children. Large groups can meet at their desks, in the center of the semicircle, or on the back rug by the big book easel. Small groups can meet on the floor, rugs, or at the back table.

Books are displayed in a number of different ways: on the wall, in crates, and on top of counters. The easiest books are displayed on the walls to show off the covers of the books. Four lines of twine are stapled into the bulletin board wall and books are attached with clothespins to the twine. These are the books that are usually used during our reading workshop activities.

Also by the book wall are the listening station and crates of books organized by themes or genres. The listening station is used before, during, and after school. Before and after school, the children can sign up to listen and read along with any recorded

Figure 3.6: My Classroom

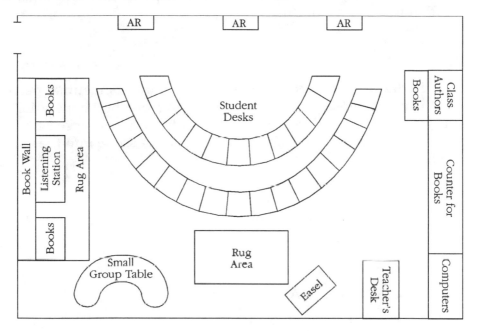

story at the station. During the school day, I choose stories from our literature anthologies or theme-related books for the children. The children listen to these books at least once a week in small groups during guided reading time. Theme books are used throughout the day with various activities.

More crates of books are placed in the front of the room for our Accelerated Reading program (AR). The crates of books are marked according to their grade level: first, second, or third grade. AR books are read at home and then children answer comprehension questions on the computer to earn points to reach a specific goal. Tests are taken throughout the day on the classroom computers. Children do not start this program until early spring when most children have become confident readers.

More sets of crates are displayed by the author bulletin board that contain books by a specific author. Student-written books are also found in this area. Books associated with science, social studies, and math concepts are displayed on counter tops. These content area books are integrated into the reading and writing curriculum whenever possible. Children are allowed to read from any of these books in the classroom when their work is completed. Some children choose to read independently and others read quietly with a partner.

Schedule

Each time period in the schedule is flexible. Sometimes periods may be shorter or longer depending on the cooperation, progress, and attention span of the children. Art, science, social studies, and math are integrated whenever possible into the language arts curriculum.

Daily Schedule

    7:45–8:00—Check in time

    8:00–8:10—Calendar

    8:10–8:35—P.E.

    * 8:35–9:00—Read Aloud

    * 9:00–9:30—Guided Reading

    * 9:30–10:05—Reader's Workshop/Independent Reading

    10:05–10:25—Recess

    * 10:25–11:00—Spelling/Phonics/Handwriting

    * 11:00–11:30—Author Study/Literature Circles

    11:30–12:12—Lunch/Recess

    * 12:12–1:00—Writer's Workshop

    1:00–1:20—Music (MWF)*Portfolios (TTh)

    1:20–2:00—Math Their Way

    2:00–2:30—Science/Social Studies

Each period marked with an asterisk (*) will be discussed in detail.

Read Aloud (20—25 minutes)

During read-aloud time, I read a variety of genres to the children. Sometimes stories are read and discussed for language, illustrations, plot, beginnings, endings, predictions, or just for pleasure. This is also a time when I read student-created books that have been published. Whenever we have extra time at the end of our read aloud, I have a student pick out a book that has been read before, and I reread it to the class. Children enjoy finding new things in the story that they missed during the first reading. Read-aloud time is an important time when children can talk about books in a low-risk environment. Daily read-alouds and talking about the reading are major components for learning in every aspect of the curriculum (Avery, 1993).

Guided Reading (30 minutes)

The roles of the teacher and children change throughout the year with guided reading. In the beginning, I start out as a model for reading, writing, speaking, listening, and viewing. I start the children out with nursery rhyme posters, wordless books, pattern books, and take-home books that supplement the K-1 literature anthologies from kindergarten. As children progress through the year, they complete five more anthologies along with take-home books for each story.

Materials

Nursery rhymes are used to relate familiar stories to the children. This helps them gain an awareness of print. I model left to right progression, one-to-one correspondence, and reading top to bottom. I also have the children look for a letter or word they know in the rhyme. If we are working on a specific letter/sound, vowel combination, or word, we look for those in the rhyme. During read-aloud time, the children may pick a rhyme to reread and talk about.

Wordless books are used to help children tell stories by using the pictures. Sometimes stories are written down and added to the books with a post-it glue stick. Wordless books (Johns & Lenski, 1997) help students develop the oral language that is needed to write stories. It also helps beginning readers start to use the picture cues that help them get ready to read words in a story.

Pattern books involve students in recognizing repetitive phrases that make stories easy to read. When students start to read these books, it is very important that they match the words they read with their fingers. This helps the children focus on the words and use one-to-one correspondence when reading. Pattern books are also good for making classroom books and retelling stories.

Take-home books and stories in the literature anthologies are short stories that start out with a repetitive pattern with one line on a page. As we go from book to book, the stories get harder and longer. Students read these books aloud in unison, with partners, and with small groups. As students become better readers, they read take-home books independently and miscues are checked during one-on-one conferences. The teacher becomes a mentor of reading instead of a model, and the child becomes an active learner.

Instruction

I use a variety of pre-reading activities with the children during guided reading time. We discuss the title and predict what the story might be about. In addition, we find known and un-known words in the story. We also view the pictures and discuss what might be happening in the story. We make semantic maps about the topic we are studying. Eventually, I pull out certain vocabulary words and have the children decide what the story may be about by reading the words. All these activities lead us to read the story to find out if our predictions are accurate.

During actual reading, I reinforce strategies that help students become independent readers. We use choral reading and partner reading. While reading, children look for picture clues, think about what makes sense, check letters/sounds to make sure they match what they are saying, and break words into smaller parts that they know. We discuss periods, commas, question marks, exclamation marks, and quotation marks.

Post-reading activities include oral retelling of the story, discussion of story grammar, a writing activity related to the story, a story map of the elements of the story, or a vocabulary worksheet. The second or third reading of a story is usually with a partner. During this time, I walk around and guide the students in their reading.

I try to use as much discussion, reading, and writing as possible. I use only a few worksheets from the literature anthologies so that students have an understanding of what is expected of them on formal tests and in the upper grades. Each story in the literature anthology is read at least twice with a choral reading by the whole class. I have the children read the story the first time to decode words and to understand the meaning of the story. The second time they read for fluency and then discuss the story grammar. Students also practice reading each story with different partners. There is also a corresponding take-home book for each story. The take-home books are read independently and then aloud. When the take-home books are finished at school, the children can take them home to practice reading to their parents.

Reading Workshop (35 minutes)

According to Carol Avery, "The heart of the reading workshop is reading" (1993, p. 323). The reading workshop period is the time when children read independently. They have the opportunity to pick their own books from the book wall to read. First, children need to be taught how to pick out a book to read. I use the theme of the three bears and tell the children that a Papa Bear book is too hard, a Mama Bear book is too easy, and a Baby Bear book is just right. Each child must find a Baby Bear book that is just right for them. Children can do this by previewing the book and trying to read the words. If a child knows all the words on the first two pages, it is a Mama Bear book, so it is a good book to read for fun but it is not challenging enough for them at this time. If a child finds five or more words that are unknown on the first two pages, it is a Papa Bear book and is too difficult to read at this time. If a child finds one to four words that are unknown on the first two pages, then this book is just right for the child to learn from. A variety of levels of books are kept on the book wall to meet the needs of all the children. When books have been read over and over or become too easy, new books are added to the wall. Children may need easier or harder books, so I show them where to find those books.

The children pick out one book each week to use for a variety of reading and writing activities throughout the week. When a child finishes with an activity, he or she may pick out another book to read. Most children read about three to four books weekly during the last ten minutes of reading workshop. To keep track of the books they read, each child records the title in a reading log after he or she has read it to a partner. The stories must be read with few errors in order to be put on a child's reading log sheet. If the stories are read fluently, the child's partner signs his or her name next to the title in the reading log. The children also write the date the story was completed. If a child doesn't read fluently, he or she is encouraged to practice and read the story again another day.

Instruction

What follows is the basic routine I use for my reading workshop. On Monday, a child picks a book that is appropriate for him or her and tries to read the book independently. I move around the room listening and giving them suggestions on how to figure out unknown words. Then the children retell their stories to a partner. New partners are picked each week. Both children then compare their stories and notice similarities or differences between their books. While children are waiting for their partners to finish reading, they draw a picture in their reading journal about any of the following things: setting, characters, problem, ending, or how the story relates to the child. What the child draws usually depends upon what was discussed during guided reading time. On Tuesday, each child reads his or her book to a partner. They then complete their drawings and write about their pictures. On Wednesday, each child shares his or her picture and writing with a partner. There is also a group sharing in front of the classroom for children who want to share. On Thursday, they talk with their partners about words that gave them problems. They then teach one another how to read each other's book. On Friday, each child checks out his or her book to read to their parents over the weekend. Any child who desires may read his or her book to the class. The class then asks the reader questions about the book that was read. If the reader doesn't know the answer, this leads to a classroom discussion with everybody answering the questions. On Monday, the books are brought back to school and reading partners have the first choice of reading the book of their partners from the week before. The "Three Bears" criteria must still apply for these books. Some children choose these books, and other children like to pick out their own books.

Conferring

The books that children usually pick out are very simple at first so this allows me to confer with each child once a week. Conferences usually last five to ten minutes. I ask students what their story is about or what they think it is about. I then listen to them read the story, giving strategies to those who need them. When we're done, I ask the children questions about how they learned to read this book. I also write down notes about the different cues that the child used to help him or her read. When the stories get longer, I have them pick out a favorite section to read to me. Possible questions to ask when they get into longer books are: Why did you pick this book? What made this part in the story special? How did the story begin or end? What was this book about? What did this story remind you of? What will you read next? Did you have any problems reading this book? How did you solve the problem or problems? This conferring time occurs throughout the year and helps me get to know each child's strengths and weaknesses.

Spelling, Phonics, and Handwriting (30 minutes)

Spelling, phonics, and handwriting are all integrated during this time period. I start the first three weeks reviewing letter names and sounds. Usually two letters are reviewed each day. The children are shown the proper way to write both uppercase and lowercase letters. Each letter has its own poster, with a specific shape on the poster as a guide for that letter sound. For example: "Aa" has a picture of an apple on it, so on this poster we would brainstorm words that begin with the letter "Aa." I try to have the children think of words that they would use when they write, so the posters can become another source for children to spell words correctly. For example, during guided reading time, we might also find words that have the "a" sound in them and write them on a list of "a" words for the children to refer to when writing. Children would also be encouraged to write an "a" word on the list if they come across one when they are reading independently.

After each letter has been reviewed, letters are combined to spell three letter words with a short vowel sound. Then words would be made up with blends, silent vowels, consonant digraphs, and special vowel combinations. I also have the children mark each word. Children put an "x" under the vowels or vowel combinations and mark the vowels short, long, or silent. They put an arc under a blend or consonant digraph. Children have a spelling test over these words weekly, along with a sentence to spell correctly. Two extra words that cannot be sounded out may be added each week to the test list. These two words would come from a list of words that the children frequently misspell in their writings. The two extra words are added to the alphabet posters on the outer edges of the shape, to be used as a reference for a word wall (Cunningham & Allington, 1994).

Other activities that we work on during this time are sentence writing and writing sprees. Both activities are used in the Reading Recovery Program (Clay, 1993b). During sentence writing, we learn to capitalize, space, and correctly spell words in a sentence. Usually, the students make up a group sentence about a story that is read during guided reading time, and then we work on making the sentence word by word. This activity is used weekly during the first semester of school.

A writing spree consists of the children writing correctly as many words as possible during a ten minute period. The teacher gives the whole class verbal prompts of words that they should know how to spell. This activity is completed once every two weeks.

Author Study/Literature Circles (35 minutes)

About every two weeks, we learn about a new author. Authors may be from the literature anthologies or authors that I have chosen who relate to the themes being studied. We learn how people become writers or illustrators, and we talk about the language that authors use in their stories and the way illustrators make their books. We also list traits that are common to their books and make comparisons to other books on the same topic. Some books are discussed in a whole group and some in small groups.

Whole Group Study

Whole group studies would be similar to read-aloud time. We compare books by the same author and discuss his or her purpose for writing them. Authors that I discuss in whole groups are: Donald Crews, Don and Audrey Wood, Tomie dePaola, Mem Fox, Julie Vivas, Jan Brett, Leo Lionni, Lois Ehlert, Patricia Polacco, Kevin Henkes, and Cynthia Rylant. The themes or styles that these authors use make them good examples for whole class discussions.

Small Group Study

Literature circles in my classroom consist of a group of four to five children who want to read the same book. I set out five books from the author we are studying and students sign up to read one of the five books. Once groups are formed, I try to have as many copies of each book as possible so each child has his or her own copy for independent activities. Next, the children decide how they want to read the book. Some groups choose reading in unison and others choose to read a page alone. At the beginning of the school year, most children read in unison, and as the year progresses, they become more independent and want to read individual pages with very little help from their peers.

The children usually take one day to read the book. Each child in the literature circle has a job to do during reading. Jobs include the book holder, the hard word recorder, the unfamiliar word recorder, and usually two word analysis helpers. The book holder holds the book and turns the pages during group reading time. This child needs to make sure that all children in the group can see the pictures and the words. As the children read the book together, the hard word recorder writes down any word that took a long time to figure out. When the children come across a word that they don't understand, the unfamiliar word recorder writes the word down. Throughout the reading of the story, the word analysis helpers remind the group what strategies to use to figure out words. If the children are stuck on a word, they can ask for teacher assistance. I walk from group to group, discussing hard or unfamiliar words that they have written down.

After the children have read the book together, they discuss the setting, characters, beginning, problem/solution, and ending. At this age, they have a hard time deciding what to discuss in detail, so I have discussion posters about each category set up around the room. On some days I have them discuss a specific poster and other days they get to make their own choice.

Questions on the Setting Poster

1. Where does the story take place? Describe it.
2. Does the author use any special words to describe the things in the setting?
3. What is the most important place in the story? Why?
4. Where else could this story take place so that the problem stays the same?
5. What other books have a setting like this book? How are the stories alike or different?

Questions on the Character Poster

1. Who are the characters in the story? Describe them.
2. Do any of the characters remind you of yourself? Who? Why?
3. How are you like the characters in this story?
4. How are you different than the characters in this story?
5. Who do the characters in this story remind you of from other stories?

Questions on the Beginning of the Story Poster

1. How does the story begin?
2. Does it grab the reader's attention? If so, how? If not, why?
3. What other stories begin like this story? Compare them.
4. How would you change the beginning of this story?

Questions on the Problem/Solution Poster

1. What is the main problem?
2. How is the problem solved?
3. Are there other problems in the story? How are they solved?
4. What are some other stories that have the same type of problem/solution? Compare them.

Questions on the End of the Story Poster

1. How did the story end?
2. Is this a good ending for the story? Why or why not?
3. What other stories end like this one? Compare them.
4. How would you change the ending of this story?

The children have been exposed to these questions during read aloud, guided reading, and reader's workshop time, so they feel very comfortable discussing these questions. I walk from group to group during this time to see how the discussion is going and guide them if their discussions have stopped. These discussions lead to whole group discussions during writer's workshop if we are working on the same part of a story in our writing.

After students discuss all areas, I have them write about a specific question from each category. One person from each circle writes about the setting, characters, beginning, problem/solution, and ending. They also have the chance to illustrate. The group then presents its information to the class. The children practice within their groups and then are graded on their presentations using a rubric. The rubric is set up into four categories: voice, organization, clearness, and content. I have the class evaluate the group and then I share my conclusions with them. This evaluation helps the children become better listeners and speakers.

These are the criteria for evaluating each category. Voice must be projected loud enough for the children in the back of the room to hear. For organization, the group members must know what they are to do once they are in front of the classroom. If a child forgets to do something, another child can help that child quietly. The material that the group presents must be clear to the audience and cover the content of what they are supposed to be presenting. The group is evaluated on whether all children, most children, some children, or few children meet the criteria. A sample rubric is shown in Figure 3.7.

When the children become confident discussing books, I have them try to persuade others to read their group's book. Students still write about the setting, characters, beginning, problem/solution, and ending, but they now have to relate it to why that particular part of the story would interest other children. After all the presentations are completed, we vote on which book they would like to read. The children cannot vote for the book they discussed. The top book is then read by the teacher during

Figure 3.7: Sample Scoring Rubric for Oral Presentations

	Group Members			
	all	most	some	few
Voice	4	3	2	1
Organization	4	3	2	1
Clearness	4	3	2	1
Content	4	3	2	1
Group Score	___/16 or ___ Percent			
Comments	_____			
	_____			

read aloud time. Children are also encouraged to read the other books that children have reported on.

Integrating Art Activities

With some of the author studies, I integrate art activities. For some Eric Carle books, we use ripped tissue paper to make our favorite character from his books. Pat Hutchins introduces us to highlighting details in our pictures with black ink. With Ezra Jack Keats' books, we use silhouettes, thinned paint, watercolors, and wallpaper to make scenes from the story. Jan Brett intrigues us with her borders and we experiment with creating original borders for our stories. Lois Ehlert uses cut-out shapes from construction paper in her illustrations, so we make small group murals using this technique. With Leo Lionni's books, we use crayon rubbings and torn wallpaper to make a large mural of *Swimmy* (1963) and the ocean creatures he meets. With Patricia Polacco's book, *The Keeping Quilt* (1988), each student makes a keeping quilt of things that are important to a child in first grade. This quilt becomes a treasured gift for parents at Christmas time.

Writer's Workshop (45 minutes)

Teacher Modeling

During the first five to ten minutes of writer's workshop, I use chart paper and write the daily news. Children volunteer things that have happened to them that day or things that they will be doing. Once our news is written, we take time to reread and look for specific letters/sounds/words. As the children become better readers, I make "mistakes" in my writing, and we go back through the chart and make corrections.

Minilessons

During the next ten minutes, we review things we have done earlier that day that can make us better writers. I do a minilesson about the content of the story, using periods, capital letters, grammar, and the overuse of certain words. Lessons change daily and are based upon the work of the children.

Writing

Before we write, I have the children brainstorm a list of possible writing topics. I give a copy of the list to each child to put in his or her writing folder. I read the list to them, and they put a dot by each topic that they might be interested in writing about. Then each child picks out a topic to write about. I encourage them to write about personal experiences and things that they know a lot about. The children usually write for about 20 minutes each day. I have noticed that if we skip a day, the children complain that they did not get to write. It is also hard for some of them to get back to writing about their topics. Donald Graves (1994) suggests that students who write daily don't have a hard time finding a topic because they are constantly thinking about what they will be writing tomorrow. The daily writing, sharing, and celebrating of writing encourages each child to become a better writer.

During writing time, I do a status of the class check to see what children are working on. Children may be writing a beginning, middle, or end to a story. Later in the year, the children may be editing a story for publication or illustrating a book.

The children write from the very first day of school. I tell them to focus on ideas and tell them not to worry about correct spelling and punctuation. Spelling and punctuation will develop later as the child becomes a better writer (Wilde, 1992). At the beginning of the year, I will see a variety of writings. Some children have random letters, some beginning or ending sounds, and a few whole words. Each child is at a different point in developmental spelling. As the child writes more, spelling and punctuation develop quickly and you can see a tremendous improvement in spelling and writing skills.

In Figure 3.8, you can see the progress Daniel made from the beginning to the end of the year. His August (8-29-95) writing reads: "I like Mrs. Waggoner. I like bunnies because they are fun to be with." His December (12-1-95) writing reads: "I want to be a writer and a illustrator. I want to draw and do art. I want to draw for people when I grow up." His April (4-18-96) writing reads: "Once upon a time there in a haunted house lived a bad monster nobody saw. It was the baddest, meanest, horrifying thing in the world. And it comes out at night and breaks in people's houses and eats food which are people! I saw it in our house. I climbed the house to my mom and dad's room to warn them. And I never saw it again."

Figure 3.8: Daniel's Writing Progress

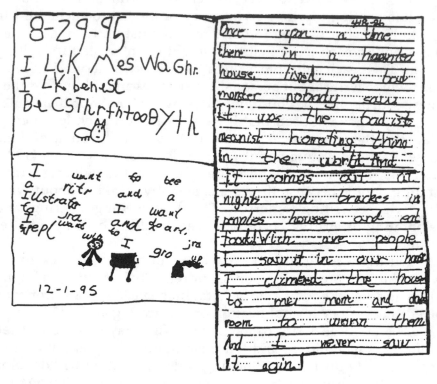

Conferring

According to Lucy Calkins, "Conferring is the heart of the writer's workshop" (1986, p. 223). This is a very important part in the development of the child's writing. I try to meet regularly with students at least once a week to discuss their writing progress and to see their successes and struggles. I do roaming conferences where I walk around the classroom and individualized conferences where the child and I are working on a specific problem. Roaming conferences last about two to three minutes and focus on getting students started with their writings. Individualized conferences last about five to ten minutes.

Publishing

By the second quarter of the year, the children have become better writers, so I have them pick out their best piece to publish. We work on the beginning, middle, and end of each story. After a child has conferred with three other children, I discuss the story with that child individually. I do not try to change his or her story, but I offer suggestions if something is unclear. Once the meaning of his or her story is clear, he or she goes over the punctuation and capitalization with three other children. Then the child confers with me again to check punctuation and capitalization. Next, the child decides if there are any spelling mistakes and circles any word he or she knows is misspelled. He or she can then confer with three more children about spelling mistakes. Children are reminded to check the alphabet posters and charts in the classroom for correct spelling of words. When the child thinks that all misspellings have been corrected, he or she gives the story to me and then I write five of the words on a sheet of paper. These words are the ones I will work on with that child to spell correctly. I discuss what sound or sounds are missing from each word and give him or her hints as to how to correct each word. The child gets two more tries to spell the word correctly before I write the correct spelling for him or her. Most children are able to accomplish the correct spelling by the second try. For the second publication, I have the children correct ten words. By the third publication, children have fewer errors and are able to start to locate words in dictionaries, so I require them to correct all words that are misspelled. The children are really excited when they start finding words in dictionaries and can correct their spelling independently.

Writing conferences begin to change when we start publishing our stories. Children sign up to meet with me for editing purposes. If I have not seen a child in a week, I will ask to meet with that child. Children may also be conferring with other children. All children still are expected to be writing about their book or another topic for at least 15 minutes.

Once the children have edited their stories, I type them and the children illustrate the story. I also have parents come in and help us with the editing and bookmaking process. When the book is completed, we have a book sharing time where the classroom author reads and discusses his or her book with the class. The children then get to take their books home to share with their families. After sharing them with their families, the books are returned and placed in the classroom library for other children to check out and read. Book publication takes children's writing out of the classroom and allows family, friends, and other children to enjoy the written work of others (Avery, 1993).

Sharing

The last ten minutes of writer's workshop is a time when the children get to share their writing in front of the class or with a partner. This is an important time that the children look forward to each day. After a child shares with the whole class, children are asked to tell things they remember about the story. They then ask questions about the writing. When children remember the details in a story, they find important gaps that lead to good questions (Graves, 1994).

Portfolios (20 minutes TTH)

Portfolios are an important part of authentically assessing the children's growth during the school year. Twice a week, children have the opportunity to review the work in their portfolio. On Tuesday, the children review their work from the previous week. After reviewing their work, they get to share their work with a partner. Children are encouraged to pick out their best work, something special, and something that they need to work on. They then discuss these three pieces with their partners. All pieces go home except for the pieces that they discussed with their partners.

On Thursday, the children take out their three pieces of work and decide which piece they will put in their first-grade portfolio. The child also stamps the date on the paper and marks the type of work that he or she has chosen. Each child has a list of different types of papers. The list includes: writing, spelling, reading, art, and math. If a child has one paper under each of the categories except math, then the child needs to pick a math paper to put in his or her portfolio. Some pieces may fit more than one category. After a child has picked a paper for the portfolio, he or she explains why it was picked. The piece that the child has picked is displayed above the book wall, where sections of the wall are divided for each child to show his or her work. The following week, the work is taken down and put into a first-grade portfolio folder that goes home with the child at the end of the year. This is a great way for parents to see the progress their child has made throughout the year. Four pieces of work are passed on to second grade. They include a writing spree, a writing sample, writing numbers to 100, and a cassette tape of their oral reading.

After each quarter of the school year, I have the children review their portfolios. I then have the students write and answer the following three questions:

1. What do you think about the work in your portfolio?
2. What did you learn this quarter?
3. What do you need to work on?

Then I confer with each child about his or her portfolio and try to set up a goal to work on for the next quarter.

A Final Word

Creating a balanced reading program takes a great deal of time, and I am still learning more things to help make my program better. Having the support of my principal and coworkers has been very helpful. While I feel my classroom program has been successful, I continue to reflect on and refine my program each year to provide the best learning opportunities and support for all of my students.

The Balanced Equation: Elementary + Secondary = A District Reading Program

Ann Kimpton

"My reading skills improved a lot because now I am actually reading books. I think that is a big improvement."

A response from a high school student on the benefits of taking a required reading class.

The development of reading skills and the need for trained reading specialists do not end after elementary school. A popular trend in secondary education is to believe that reading instruction is the exclusive domain of the elementary school. Although it would be nice to believe that all reading problems could be solved if overcome in the early grades, the truth of the matter is that middle and high schools have students who need the assistance of reading teachers. Part of the solution in creating a balanced reading program is to include secondary reading instruction in the equation.

The definition of what constitutes a middle or high school reading program varies from school district to district. Secondary schools may claim that content area teachers are capable of and are willing to spend class time teaching higher-level reading strategies; however, few content teachers see the need to devote precious class time to developing reading skills. Due to lack of training, many teachers do not know how to teach reading strategies, and some naively assume that, by their age, students should have acquired the skills necessary to be fluent readers of their texts. Acknowledging the significance of secondary reading teachers by designating a specific place for reading in the curriculum is another way schools can move toward balance. A district that professes to offer a reading program taught solely by content area teachers is one that is overlooking the realities of today's classrooms.

Frequently, if a high school does offer a reading program, that instruction may be limited to disabled readers. The perception that reading instruction is only necessary for remediation is much too narrow. If reading instruction is vital to intellectual growth, students should continue reading instruction through high school, even those students regarded as average to above-average. It is to these students that the third tenet of a balanced reading equation is addressed: students in the middle can and will benefit from specific instruction in reading.

Balance in Action at Willowbrook High School

Willowbrook High School (WHS) in Villa Park, Illinois, is an example of a balanced reading program addressing needs at the high school level. Situated in suburban Chicago, this high school serves a diverse, ethnically-mixed population of approximately 1,800 students. The Reading Department is led by an energetic educator, Roberta Sejnost, who has made it her life's commitment to ensure the growth in reading abilities of all of Willowbrook's students.

Willowbrook offers a corrective reading program to students reading below grade level. A unique feature of Willowbrook's commitment to reading is a graduation requirement that all students reading at or above grade level take a semester course called Advanced Reading Strategies (ARS).

Balance in the Classroom

The reading lab is a spacious classroom overlooking the school tennis courts. As the students file into the room, they head to a row of vertical wooden racks, grab a vinyl packet, and sit at their assigned tables. The lab has eleven rectangular tables spread throughout the room at various angles, with three students assigned to each table. The teacher's desk is in the middle of the room and a desk for the reading lab aide is to the side. Wire rotating book racks, displaying an array of genres, including mystery, adventure, classic literature, sports, biography, and current best sellers, dot the four corners of the room. Bean bags, carpet squares, and pillows are casually tossed along two sides of the classroom. The other classroom walls are lined with 25 computers. Overall, the impression is that this is a room where reading is enjoyable and a priority.

Daily Schedule

As the bell rings, all of the students are seated. Each has taken a self-selected novel from his or her vinyl packet and has begun to read. Every class period begins with sustained silent reading (SSR). For the next 15 minutes, the students are engrossed in their novels. The routine has been well established, so no one questions what to do. Marilyn Payton, the second period teacher, also reads a novel. At the end of the time, she announces the daily journal prompt. Students take from the packet a spiral notebook and begin responding to the prompt, "If your book were a flavor, what would it be and why?" Again a daily routine has been firmly established as students note the date, book title, and pages read at the beginning of each journal entry.

After the students complete the entry, Mrs. Payton announces the class activity for the day. On some days, the class as a whole participates in one group activity, but today half of the class is practicing rate instruction on computers and the other half is receiving small group instruction in semantic mapping at tables at the far end of the room. The reading aide has loaded the computer programs and each student's computer log is at his or her assigned computer. Progress is recorded on the log. While Mrs. Payton works with the smaller group, the aide assists students on the computers.

A few minutes before the end of the 50 minute class period, students put their materials back into the vinyl packets and place them back in the wooden racks, returning to their original tables. Voices buzz about the next novel they will read. The bell rings and the students leave. Balance in the daily schedule allows for individual reading, whole class or small group instruction, and individual or group skill practice.

Balance in the Curriculum

Advanced Reading Strategies provides a balance of instruction in developmental, functional, and recreational reading. SSR allows busy high school students the opportunity for pleasure reading, time that few students are able or willing to make.

Instruction in pre-, during-, and post-reading strategies is emphasized. Students learn to identify text structures, select the main idea, distinguish fact and opinion, and develop inferencing and other critical thinking skills. Improvement in study skills, specifically note taking, test taking, organization, and memory strategies are addressed during the semester. Part of the study skills unit involves identifying student learning styles and learning strategies. This helps students cope with the strengths and weaknesses of each particular style. Other parts of the curriculum focus on vocabulary and developing a flexible reading rate. The balance among the three areas is an essential component in the success of the WHS program.

Technology allows the diverse ARS curriculum to be adapted to an individual level. During computer time, students develop skills in rate, comprehension, reasoning, and vocabulary. Favorite software compatible with Apple or Macintosh hardware includes the following programs: "Speed Reader II" for rate; "Comprehension Power" or "Mindscape's Reading Workshop" for comprehension; "The Lost R" and "Mind Castle I and II" for reasoning; and "Quantum," which ties comprehension activities to the *Word Clues* vocabulary books.

Balanced Assessment

Balance is also necessary in assessment. Students are assessed in a variety of ways from the traditional to the more holistic. In today's high schools, grades are important. Teachers are held accountable to justify each grade given; therefore, all areas of the balanced program are a part of the grade assigned to each student. Students are required to complete two book conferences per quarter, but they are given a choice of the type of conference they wish to complete. The element of choice eases the punitive aspect of a book report; granted, it would be wonderful if all students would read for pure enjoyment, but in the real world of competing interests and grades, this may be the next best thing. Books are also self-selected, which contributes to greater student satisfaction.

Conference options range from a teacher-student conference, parent-student, or student-student conference, to more creative approaches. Students may illustrate a favorite scene, make a "Dear Abby" audiotape of one of the character's problems, or create a video. This variety gives students many opportunities to express their comprehension of a particular book. Additionally, student journals are collected for teacher comments every two weeks, and students are assessed on the content and quality of their daily responses to the writing prompts.

Over the course of the semester, students complete a study skills project which focuses on improving skills in a class in which they would like to improve. Each student keeps a log of events from that particular class and analyzes how the direct instruction from ARS affects achievement in the class. By the end of the project, the majority of students have seen the explicit benefit of instruction in areas of test taking, note taking, organization, and memory skills.

Grades for students are also based on vocabulary development at the student's individual level, computer credit earned for working independently and completing a computer log, and daily assignments.

Roberta Sejnost has found portfolio assessment effective in her ARS class. Each student keeps a three-ring binder which serves as a dynamic record of his or her progress in reading. ARS portfolios contain both individual test results and student reflections on those results. Additionally, students devise action plans to capitalize on their reading strengths while they develop strategies to compensate for areas of need. Other sections of the portfolio include note taking samples, a chart of reading rate improvement, and book discussion reflections. At the end of the semester, Mrs. Sejnost confers with each student individually to determine the final portfolio contents. The student selects five samples representative of his or her best work, to which Mrs. Sejnost adds the five samples she has chosen. Two further samples are added by a peer or a parent to complete the collection. By the end of the semester, each student portfolio serves as concrete evidence of the progress gained from Mrs. Sejnost's ARS class.

Results of a Balanced Reading Program

At the beginning and the end of every semester, students in ARS are given the Blue Level of the *Stanford Diagnostic Reading Test* (Karlsen & Gardner, 1984). The results of these entrance and exit scores are then compared to track evidence of student growth. Each student's pre- and post-scores are plotted on an individual bell curve and the results are shared with parents. A longitudinal study of ARS students from 1991 to 1995 showed an average student gain of two grade levels in vocabulary and comprehension during the course of the semester, as measured by the *Stanford Diagnostic Reading Test*. This evidence of student growth is necessary to justify the existence of this program to constituents concerned about quantifying results. The results of these assessments concretely demonstrate the effectiveness of the ARS program.

Student Perceptions of a Balanced Program

Part of the balance of a secondary reading program is the opportunity for student voices to be heard. At the end of the spring 1996 semester, 125 students were surveyed about the ARS program. The results are very telling.

Students were asked to respond to the open prompt, "What was the most valuable part of this class for you?" Their reactions then were tallied and organized into categories. As some students cited multiple reasons in their answers to a single question, the total number of responses and students does not always match. See Table 3-1. Repeatedly, students emphasized the value of learning strategies that teachers often assume they have learned by the time they reach high school: "The most valuable part of the class for me was the note taking because I've always hated outlines and now I know other ways to take notes that are more interesting."

Table 3-1: Student Responses to Most Valuable Part of Reading Class

Area Identified	Number of Responses
Developing note taking skills	36
The opportunity to read for pleasure in school	31
Computer reading and vocabulary programs	17
Improvement in study skills	16
Learning to read faster	15
Vocabulary growth	11
Book conferences	7
Miscellaneous	6
Total responses:	139

   Even book conferences were seen as beneficial by students as a reading incentive: "The most valuable part of this class for me, I think, were the book reports. If it were up to me, I wouldn't have read any books this year. Because of this reading class I read eight books! I even found an author I like, so book reports were very valuable to me."

   Allowing class time for pleasure reading is also critical to the development of lifelong readers. These comments give us pause to reflect on the importance of allowing students time to read for pleasure in school.

- "I don't normally read outside school. I have always had trouble reading, and this class really helped. I enjoy reading more outside the class now."

- "The most valuable part of this class was to get me reading again. I used to always read, but for some reason, I stopped."

   Another survey question asked students to, "Describe how your reading skills have improved this year." Student responses are listed in Table 3-2.

   Most students saw multiple benefits of the ARS course:

- "My reading skills have flourished. I'm reading a lot faster, and I can understand the material. I've also gotten into the habit of reading for pleasure."

Table 3-2: Student Responses to How Their Reading Skills Improved

Area Identified	Number of Responses
Reading rate	93
Comprehension	42
Read more for pleasure/positive attitude toward reading	24
Note taking skills	11
Vocabulary	8
Miscellaneous	5
Total responses:	183

Students also recognized that to become better readers, they have to read more often:

- "The speed of my reading has improved this year because of the practice I've been getting. Also, I have read more books this year that I would not have read unless I had this class."

Even the smallest step toward independent reading was viewed as a success:

- "It has gotten me to read, and that is improvement enough. Matter of fact, I'm even reading a book right now for my own entertainment."

Giving students the opportunity for pleasure reading may be a link to creating future adults who read:

- "My reading skills have improved greatly this year because before this year I did not like to read at all and now I do. It [Sustained Silent Reading] got me to read more even out of school. I usually never read. That made me actually enjoy reading."

The overwhelming message implicit in these student voices is that given the opportunity to read, students will find reading enjoyable. And the more teens read, the better readers they will become.

Hope for the Future of Secondary Reading Programs

As society becomes more technologically advanced, the demands upon the typical high school reader will increase. Students will have to read on a much higher level in the workplace as jobs requiring only low-level literacy move beyond the borders of the United States. The average student in today's American secondary schools is often neglected. Programs are in place to help struggling students through Title I or remedial programs, and gifted students, especially in suburban schools, have the opportunity for advanced placement classes or community college courses. Little assistance, however, is available for the student who must work hard to earn a "C" and who most likely will not attend an Ivy League school. Schools must commit to these students who have so much to offer and will form the backbone of this nation's future citizenry. Reading programs for these students will not only support their literacy development, but they will be instrumental in creating lifelong advocates of literacy.

Close Up—
A Collage of Issues

The unifying aspect of the articles in this section is that they all deal with a close up focus on particular issues. The articles address the issues of inclusion, the whole language versus phonics debate, assessment, and technology. These articles highlight both challenges and suggestions for addressing those challenges.

The recent emphasis on inclusion programs has created new relationships among professionals who may not have worked together closely in the past. Many teachers are placed in new organizational schemes without much preparation or input. In this sense, many Title 1 reading teachers must struggle with balance from two perspectives: within the reading program and between "push-in and pull-out" reading services.

With the recent media attention pitting whole language against phonics instruction, the struggle of one teacher to come to grips with the notion of whole language and skills (especially phonics) provides a timely glimpse into what many teachers are currently experiencing. While the author's position clearly leans toward phonics, her quest to integrate the language arts illustrates a different aspect of balanced reading instruction.

Assessment and technology are two additional areas that are likely to challenge and frustrate teachers. Assessment has long been a source of concern to teachers. Many teachers feel caught between the call for more authentic assessments and the increased emphasis on state and local standardized assessments. In this section, a relatively new teacher describes how she attempts to balance assessment, especially the roles of students and parents, in her classroom. The two articles on technology provide a glimpse into how classrooms in the 21st century might be changed by computers and other technology. After reflecting on the ideas shared, consider how classrooms might be enhanced by technology and also consider new challenges which may result from the increased use of technology.

The Challenge of Balanced Reading Instruction for In-Class Special Reading Programs

Mary Kelly

It's hard to be a classroom reading teacher and stay on the right side of what is currently accepted as the best way to teach reading. Do you go with a literature-based program and assume that students will somehow intuitively figure out how to turn letter symbols into sounds and words? Do you use a whole language approach because someone in the administration has mandated this approach, but sneak phonics instruction into your program because your experience tells you that students need direct instruction in word identification strategies despite what some "experts" lead you to believe? Or do you continue with a traditional basal reading program with an emphasis on skills and assume that the students will read enough outside of school to develop a love for words and a passion for literature on their own? If it's difficult for a classroom reading teacher to decide which is the best way to design a reading program, it is even more complicated for the reading specialist who operates with much higher stakes—the teaching of reading to our most fragile group: struggling readers. Adding to the complexity of this already difficult decision is the fact that many specialists service struggling readers within the context of another teacher's classroom in what is commonly called a "push-in" or "in-class" program.

Because of the enormous responsibility that goes with teaching students to read, it is imperative that all teachers choose research-supported methods that best help children learn to read. Despite much variation in what is going on in classrooms, I believe that for most children an eclectic or balanced approach that combines the teaching of word recognition skills, strategies for comprehending what one reads, and improving one's motivation to read is the best.

In this article, I describe a framework of balanced instruction that I use as a middle school reading specialist. Although my experience is at the sixth, seventh, and eighth grade level, I think this basic outline of how to provide in-class reading help to struggling readers could be applied to lower and higher grades as well. I see this framework as an overlay to be put on top of the regular reading teacher's program. What I mean is that struggling readers can follow the regular reading class when two conditions are met: 1) when the regular classroom work is appropriate for their needs; and 2) when some provision is made for specific instruction in their areas of need. It is important that the reading specialist provide a balanced program for the students in his or her care despite what the classroom teacher may be doing. By alternating between small group and whole class instruction with his or her students, the reading specialist can ensure that balance occurs.

The year I was hired as a middle school reading specialist was the year my school district became a "full inclusion" district, with all special services provided within the classroom. At the time, there was not much research to support the efficacy of this new model or to provide guidelines to teachers. We created our own models as we went along.

My transition to this new type of reading program was easy for several reasons. First, the administration had made it very clear that full inclusion was the only goal. Any pull-out, no matter how minimal, was not considered to be in the students' best interests. At the same time, most of the other school districts in the area had changed to the same in-class model of reading support. We were with the majority. I was also fortunate in this new venture because all of the teachers with whom I collaborated accepted me as a co-teacher right from the start. Finally, the students and the parents were happy with the program. The parents' perception was that their children were receiving extra help, but in a way that did not make them appear different or singled out.

Everyone was happy, except me. Despite what appeared to be my initial success in delivering in-class reading support to struggling readers, I began to ask myself if this was truly the best way to improve students' reading. True, the students were happy, their parents were happy, and the administration was happy. However, the bottom line was not if everyone was happy, but if the students were truly improving their reading.

I began to examine closely both my role in the class and the methods I was using. Depending on the lesson, I seemed to swing between high-priced teacher's aide and co-teacher with full responsibility for the entire class. This arrangement did not leave much time for addressing the specific needs of the struggling readers. The problem was compounded by the fact that many reading specialists, myself included, began using adaptations and methods used by special education teachers. We read difficult books to students or had them listen to taped versions. In effect, we were trying to improve students' reading by not having them read, flying in the face of research linking the amount of reading with proficiency in reading (Allington, 1977). Clearly, my reading program had become imbalanced.

In an effort to bring some balance back, I had to first define what a balanced remedial program would look like. A synthesis of several researchers' work lead me to conclude that the major areas of a remedial program are: 1) word recognition, 2) comprehension, 3) use of metacognitive reading strategies, 4) vocabulary, and 5) motivation to read (Barr, Blachowicz, & Wogman-Sadow, 1995; Johns, VanLeirsburg, & Davis, 1994; Kibby, 1995; Manzo & Manzo, 1993; Stahl & Pickle, 1996). I suggest that these areas are the components of a balanced reading program. To balance my reading program, students' needs in each of these areas must be addressed, and not ignored, in the interest of keeping everyone in the same book, on the same page, or in the same class. Keeping students' needs as readers as the focus of the program may sound obvious, but it is the first step in making sure the program does not get out of balance.

To make sure I address the students' needs in the most efficient way possible, I have become much more flexible in how that instruction is delivered. I no longer try to provide remedial services only within the context of the regular reading class. Instead, I choose the type of instruction to match the need, and I teach small groups in and out of the class, also working with students one-to-one.

The second thing I have done to get my program more balanced is to develop an ongoing system of assessing students' progress in each of the areas that make up a good reading program. What follows is a detailed explanation of how I assess and monitor students' growth in reading in a remedial program that is based within the regular reading class.

Assessing and Monitoring Word Recognition

I begin the year with some testing to help me get a baseline of where to begin with students. First, I have a standardized reading test score from the previous spring from the *Degrees of Reading Power* (Touchstone Applied Science Associates, 1995). Next, I administer the *Basic Reading Inventory (BRI)* (Johns, 1994) to each student. The *BRI* gives me a good idea of how many students are still in need of work in word recognition and fluency.

After the *BRI* has been administered, I tape record each student reading an instructional-level passage. Two more times during the school year—after the first semester and at the end of the year—I tape them reading the same passage. Students listen to the tape with me and we do a miscue analysis together, discussing the graphophonemic, syntactic, and semantic fit of the miscue, and whether or not the miscue was corrected. We then record this information on a miscue analysis chart.

For most of my students, that is enough. For students who are still experiencing difficulty in upper-level word identification strategies, I do a miscue analysis on a more regular basis, using the material that they are reading in class. Students who do not read fluently do timed repeated readings (see Johns & Lenski, 1997), again using a portion of the material being read in class for the readings.

Another way I have provided word recognition help is to give a focus lesson using selected words from the story prior to the students' reading of the story. I choose multisyllabic words that I think will cause the student some difficulty. I underline the potentially difficult word and present it in context. While students are decoding the word, I have them do a "think-aloud," telling me how they are going about figuring out the word.

I have discovered that the key to providing word recognition help in an in-class program is to keep the focus lessons short enough so that the student can be returned to the classroom within a few minutes, thus avoiding problems with him or her missing an entire lesson or having to make up work that was missed. Using the text being read in class as the text for the focus lesson keeps the lesson authentic.

It is important that middle school reading specialists do not neglect word recognition difficulties. Because many sixth, seventh, and eighth graders do not have problems in this area, word recognition is not usually a part of the curriculum at this level. It becomes easy, therefore, to let students with this problem slip through the cracks. The reading specialist needs to integrate word recognition into the regular reading class for those who need it through out-of-class instruction or one-on-one instruction if necessary. Ignoring this area of reading results in an imbalance in instruction.

To monitor students' progress, I keep a documentation portfolio with a section for each of the five areas that I have identified as part of a balanced remedial reading program. In the word recognition section, each student has a cassette tape on which he or she has read the same passage three times during the year. Students who need further work in word identification also have copies of miscue analyses and graphs of timed repeated readings. This documentation is used to help set goals for the student and as a means for measuring his or her progress toward these goals.

Assessing and Monitoring Comprehension

For struggling middle school readers, comprehension is the area of biggest concern. Reading difficult text to students or putting it on tape, while commonly used techniques, do more to improve students' listening skills than reading skills. The question is, what can be done to help students understand what they are reading when the bulk of the instruction is done in a regular classroom using materials that are usually at a frustration level for the student?

The first step in helping struggling readers to better comprehend what is being read is to start with the classroom teacher. During our weekly planning sessions, I suggest activities that can be used to facilitate everyone's comprehension. I make sure that the lesson includes pre-reading activities which build the background knowledge my students are often missing and that enough time is allowed for my students to finish the story. If they need more time, I will often eliminate one of the post-reading activities for my students and allow them extra time for reading and clarification.

Because of the collaborative nature of an in-class program, I want to stress that cooperation and mutual respect between the reading specialist and the classroom teacher are the crux of a successful program. I have found it best if I start out assuming that all students will be successful with the teacher's lesson plans. Next, I look at the plan to decide where struggling readers will have problems and make adaptations or provide special focus lessons. To collaborate successfully, both teachers need to be committed to spending time outside of class in preparation and planning.

The second method I use to closely monitor students' comprehension is to do frequent checks to see if they are understanding their reading. For each novel that is taught, I keep a set of index cards with questions for each chapter. When the students are reading, I unobtrusively move around the room, asking students some of these questions. This helps me be aware of how well they're understanding or if they're even reading. It also enables me to answer questions or clarify things before a student becomes helplessly lost. I can do this immediately on an individual basis, or if a number of students are not understanding, I can pull those students out to re-read the chapter they found confusing. I also ask students to do a retelling of what they've read.

Perhaps the best method I have found to improve students' comprehension in an inclusion program is to teach an alternative book to the struggling readers. When the novel being read by the class is at the frustration level for my students, I either choose a similar novel at a more appropriate level, or I do a reader's workshop with my students based on the genre or theme of the book being read by the rest of the class. These are both highly successful alternatives to dragging struggling readers through a book that is too difficult for them. As Adams (1990) points out, "There is evidence that achievement in reading is improved by placement in materials that a student can read with a low error rate (2 percent to 5 percent), and that students placed in materials that they read with greater than 5 percent errors tend to be off-task during instruction" (p. 113). To assess the readability of a certain book, I develop a cloze passage from the book and have students complete it prior to reading the book. A nice benefit to using an alternative novel is that students who are given a novel at an appropriate level usually find the reading experience enjoyable, and they exhibit a positive attitude.

A fourth way of dealing with struggling readers in the area of comprehension is to teach focus lessons. Often, I will pull a small group out for brief pre-reading lessons or for re-reading certain parts of a story. As with word recognition lessons, the key to success lies in making the lesson focused and brief, so as not to have students away from the classroom for a whole class period.

To monitor students' progress in comprehension, I keep classwork that assesses comprehension in the students' portfolio. Examples can include answers to questions, quizzes, journal responses to literature, story maps, retellings, and cloze passages. The students and I use all of these documents at the end of each quarter to evaluate progress toward the goal of understanding what is read.

Assessing and Monitoring Use of Strategies

To determine whether or not my students are strategic readers, I give them all the *Metacomprehension Strategy Index* (Schmitt, 1990; found in Johns & Lenski, 1997) at the beginning of the year. This is a multiple-choice questionnaire in which students complete sentences about what they do while they are reading. The teacher uses the results to evaluate strategic awareness in students.

As with comprehension, my first step in providing instruction to my students in strategic reading is to work with the classroom teacher to include explicit instruction of strategies as part of the whole class lesson. During our weekly planning sessions, I suggest ways that we can teach the process of reading as well as the content of the story. Many times I will teach the class a focus lesson emphasizing a certain strategy. Some examples of comprehension strategies that I teach are purpose-setting, predicting and verifying, self-questioning, connecting the story to one's experience, summarizing, self-monitoring of comprehension, and the need for flexible reading rates. Monitoring a student's use of strategies can be done in class while the students are working. I will stop at their desks and ask them to predict what will happen next or ask them if there are any parts of the story they did not understand, and what they did if they did not understand.

To provide extra help for my students, I sometimes do a short lesson on how to read the story or how to use a strategy. These lessons are done at the beginning of class while the classroom teacher is doing something organizational or conducting a pre-reading activity. My students then return to the class to begin reading the story with the rest of the class.

To help assess students' growth in strategic reading, I do two things each quarter. First, the students and I look at the papers in the comprehension section of their portfolio to determine whether an improvement in strategic reading occurred. I also have the students fill out a self-assessment on how often they think they use certain strategies.

Assessing and Monitoring Vocabulary Skills

Vocabulary development is the fourth area of reading that I monitor in my reading program. To provide as much instruction as I can within the framework of the regular reading class, I start with the classroom teacher. During our weekly planning sessions, I make sure that vocabulary is not overlooked in the reading lesson. Often I plan and teach that part of the lesson because many of the teachers with whom I co-teach do not have reading backgrounds.

To provide individual help to struggling readers, I take them in a small group to discuss the vocabulary words they are being taught. This helps them get a deeper understanding of the words. I also target phrases and idioms in the material being read that might be problematic for my students and give them a quick focus lesson on these words before they read.

To assess vocabulary development, I put any work that measures understanding of words in the vocabulary section of each student's portfolio. These papers are looked at once a quarter collaboratively with the student to determine if the grades indicate that progress is being made in vocabulary.

Assessing and Monitoring Motivation to Read

A balanced reading program needs to address not only how competent a reader is but how avid a reader he or she is. As the U.S. Commission on Reading reported in *Becoming a Nation of Readers*, "Increasing the proportion of children who read widely and with evident satisfaction ought to be as much a goal of reading instruction as increasing the number who are competent readers" (Anderson, Hiebert, Scott, & Wilkinson, 1985, p. 15). I think that encouraging a love of reading and increasing a student's experience with print are goals that are as important as improving their ability to read.

In the beginning of the year, I give students a reading attitude scale (Estes, 1971; found in Johns & Lenski, 1997) to see how they feel about reading. I also add an interest survey to see what kinds of books or topics students would be interested in reading.

With my own students, I use their interest surveys to make specific suggestions for books. Students also keep a log of books they have read in their portfolios.

Encouraging a love of reading is a goal that can be easily worked on in an inclusion setting because most students need to be turned on to the pleasure of reading. I frequently do book talks with the whole class on good young adult books that I've read. Regular reading of *Booklist, The Alan Review,* and *The Journal of Adolescent & Adult Literacy* has provided me with great suggestions for books. I am preparing a collection of these book reviews that students can peruse to find books that may interest them.

Finding good books and encouraging reading for pleasure are only half of the solution in motivating problem readers to read. It has been my experience that many struggling readers not only don't read for pleasure, but many of them do not read regular class assignments. As part of their quarterly assessment, I analyze the percentage of assignments completed and assignments turned in late. Their goal is to increase this percentage as the year goes on.

Closing Thoughts

Is it possible to provide remedial help to struggling readers in an in-class setting? I think it is if the teacher does not let the program become imbalanced. To keep instruction balanced, the needs of the students must always be the main focus of the program. Blind adherence to a policy of inclusion cannot be the guiding force. The reading specialist must be aware of each student's needs and decide what is the best method for meeting those needs, whether it be whole class, small group, or individual instruction.

Is it a good idea to provide remedial help to struggling readers in an in-class setting? I think the benefits of being in a class where the average level of achievement is higher than in a remedial pull-out class, and no stigma is attached to receiving extra help, can be a terrific benefit—but only if the reading specialist keeps the program balanced and does not let the inclusive nature of the program stand in the way of instruction.

Balanced Reading:
Notions, Emotions, and Potions

Beth R. Cowman

Until recently, I have been blissfully ignorant of the surging controversy between the "traditionalists" and the "whole language luminaries." I am a tried and true traditionalist, tucked away in the rural community of Winnebago, Illinois. The concept of whole language has drifted out to us in professional magazines and other educational literature, but we left that "experiment" to be carried out in nearby Rockford where they are bolder and more "cutting edge." Let them find the "land mines," and we'll come along and pick up the pieces.

During a recent workshop, emphasis was placed on a very common principle in all of life—namely, *balance*. It is through this exposure that I am motivated to research and implement more concepts that are commonly called whole language into my daily traditional reading instruction.

Notions

A major inhibitor to the acceptance of whole language by the traditional teacher is that no one seems to know exactly what it involves. The notion of whole language is obviously ambiguous, perhaps purposefully so, because it embraces a whole host of notions. According to Chall (1996), P. David Pearson views whole language in opposition to the use of basal readers.

> *Others place whole language on the side of reading whole books,*
> *particularly literature as opposed to short selections in basal*
> *reader texts; still others focus on the non-teaching of reading*
> *skills by whole language and that instead skills are to be inferred*

from reading connected texts. For others, whole language means empowering teachers to teach reading as they think best. For still others, it means integrating the teaching of reading with writing, speaking, and listening. For a growing number, it means a philosophy of education and of life, not merely a method of teaching reading. It is, therefore, difficult to discuss whole language since its meaning may differ from person to person, and even includes, in some schools, teaching phonics and using basal readers as components of a whole language program (Chall, 1996, unnumbered introduction).

Nevertheless, there are some valuable observations, concepts, and methods espoused by whole language enthusiasts that must be considered and set into motion.

I must admit, when I first learned of the whole language concept and the ensuing debate, I thought, what's the controversy? Reading proficiency involves both word recognition and meaning. But I soon discovered that the flap seems to be over which should come first: meaning or phonics. Of what value is it to teach children a host of phonics rules when meaning is the real purpose of reading and writing? My question and that of phoneticians is, "What good is knowing what a word means if you cannot recognize the word when you see it, because you cannot decode the letters?"

My reconciliation of this emotional issue involves personal introspection and observation. Perhaps there is authoritative testimony elsewhere, but I have yet to encounter it. As I mentioned earlier, I am somewhat new to the debate scene. Whole language is of primary importance when considering the listening and speaking aspects of literacy. Common sense observation tells us that a baby hears whole language and begins to accumulate an inventory of whole words. Parents don't rehearse the sounds of each letter in the alphabet with their infants or go over word meanings, but the child learns to associate the whole words and sentences with other sensory stimuli to gain meaning. Consequently, the baby's mind is "programmed" through whole language and meaning.

Speaking follows listening, and, if a baby could, it would probably speak in the whole words and sentences that it has heard. As the baby develops, it does start to speak whole words and even whole sentences. My youngest son, Daniel, was speaking with whole words and complex sentences at nine months. I believe this is because he was "immersed" in language by his parents, siblings, and babysitter. While I realize that this example may seem obvious, it is fundamental to my philosophy of reading instruction.

Unlike listening and perhaps speaking, learning to read and write requires a rational process of identifying words by combining the individual sounds associated with its letters. Granted, it is possible to associate meanings with whole groups of letters, but, over time, the memorization required of even the most mentally adept person would be staggering. The old dilemma that we've all been in comes to mind. The student asks his teacher how to spell a word and the teacher says, "Look it up in the dictionary." But how can the student do that if he or she doesn't have some idea of how to spell it? Many of the newest dictionaries boast of up to 200,000 words, and without a working knowledge of orthography, a student will not have a clue about spelling or decoding a word that he or she has never seen written before. If the student is equipped with a phonics background, he or she may not locate the word right away, but will at least have a chance (through trial and error) of finding it.

Phonics, of course, is not a panacea. The honest phonics teacher will have to admit that the English language has many exceptions to phonic rules. Phonics, however, can often get the reader close to a word's pronunciation. This is where that inventory of words learned early in life comes into play. Phonics gets you close to the proper identification, but the mind must make the jump from close to "right on" by searching the memory for the exact pronunciation and meaning. How the brain does this, no one really knows. "Because reading processes are internal, diagnosticians have been left to infer what is going on in a reader's head" (Henk, 1993, p. 109). Nevertheless, the brain needs a few clues in order to lock onto the correct word the eyes are viewing. Phonics is one of the best prompters available. From my point of view, phonics and whole language should go together, hand-in-glove.

It seems to me that the crux of comprehension is analysis and reasoning. In other words, one needs both the ability to dissect the whole and see the parts, and then put it back together through reasoning. A case in point happened when I tried to digest Henk's observation of the transformation that has taken place in reading education: "No longer is effective reading ability considered to be the aggregate of a large number of separate, specific, and measurable subskills. Instead, facile reading is now perceived as the holistic orchestration of related strategic processes that lead to constructing meaning from a text" (Henk, 1993, p. 103). I had little difficulty in understanding that first sentence, but the second one proved more difficult. Fortunately, I have a method for decoding the sentence: taking it apart word by word, looking up needed words in the dictionary, noting the various meanings, and then, by trial and error, reconstructing the sentence to grasp the meaning. The current trend for defining a good reader is the ability to interrelate all of the needed processes in order to produce meaning from what is being read. Without this decoding method, I would be lost.

Even though it is reassuring to learn that books such as *Learning to Read: The Great Debate* (Chall, 1996) reinforce what most of us traditionalists know by common sense and intuition, I can see a need to be aware of objections and criticisms raised by whole language proponents. Consider the "fish" adage: "Give a person a fish and he or she will eat for a day. Teach a person to fish and he or she will eat for a lifetime." Whole language advocates would say that if you give a student enough fish, he will learn to fish as a by-product of eating fish. On the other hand, the traditionalists could smugly say, "Teach a person to fish and he or she will eat for a lifetime!" But a legitimate whole language response would be, what if the student hates fish? Or, what if he or she becomes so belabored with casting skills, bait assortments, kinds of fish, types of fishing locations, and so on, that he or she never puts the line in the water? Balanced fishing, like balanced reading, would include *both* giving and teaching. After giving someone a fish, see if he or she liked it. Then show the student how you got it, and teach the student what goes into fishing. Similarly, expose students to authentic literature by reading orally and discussing meaning, morals, emotions, and so on. See if they like the story. Then teach them the skills that a good reader uses, while frequently relating the individual skills to each other (phonics to spelling, etc.) and referring often to the authentic literature. If skill troubles develop with authentic literature, inject quality instruction. By recognizing the strengths and weaknesses of both sides of the debate, we can forget the rhetoric and make a motion toward balance!

Motions and Emotions

What motions should be taken? In view of the increasing and overwhelming research supporting phonics instruction (Chall, 1996), the whole language extremists should admit that meaning without phonics produces a higher incidence of failure. The traditionalist, on the other hand, should admit that some of the whole language concepts would be beneficial if integrated properly with phonics instruction. Both sides should make motions toward the middle to achieve balance. Unfortunately, this is not likely to happen. The resistance is not based on logic or reasoning, but on emotions. I am sure that many traditionalists are stubbornly ignoring the whole language ideas without even examining them. I must admit that my recent experience in a graduate reading course has changed my view of whole language. I'm willing to alter my instructional procedures to incorporate some whole language concepts into a strong phonics-based foundation. I realize that in order to compete with the multitude of visual distractions vying for my students' reading attention, I must be flexible enough to add some authentic literature and more teacher read-aloud time.

I am particularly dismayed to learn from Jeanne Chall that emotions are winning out over logic to the detriment of students.

> The professional literature of the past decade appears to be less reasoned than that in earlier periods. This is an ironic twist since the research and theoretical evidence on beginning reading today is much stronger than it was in the earlier periods. The debates of 1983 to 1993 tend also to use stronger language, and seem to be grounded more in ideology and emotion than on available scientific and theoretical evidence. The strong rhetoric and ideological base have led more than one journalist to call the current debates "reading wars" (Chall, 1996, unnumbered introduction).

The culprits here are emotions, which add to the ironies of the situation. Meaning-emphasis methods, it seems, were readily adopted under the well-meaning "values of love, care, and concern for children" (Chall, 1996, unnumbered introduction). Unfortunately, these children end up failing at a higher rate! In spite of the mounting evidence against comprehension-emphasis approaches, misplaced altruistic emotions cause these methods of instruction to persist. "Whole language, in particular, seems to say that a good heart goes a long way, and that a desire to learn to read is the strongest factor in learning. Its major concern is that the child be motivated to want to learn to read and that the higher cognitive processes be used in reading right from the start. It flees from the idea that there may be 'basics' to be learned first" (Chall, 1996, unnumbered introduction).

It is my belief that no matter how much someone wants to read, he or she cannot overcome the natural processes of mental development. It is because I care for my students that I put them through the rigors of phonics instruction. The instruction lasts for only a year or two, but the benefits of a keen reading ability last for a lifetime! You might call it "tough love." Although I believe in a tough phonics discipline, I can see a need to establish a successful literacy-oriented classroom. Every solid foundation should have a nice structure built on it.

Potions

My goal is to have a healthy "patient" through holistic medicine. My guiding "prescription" is to accomplish literacy by interrelating listening, speaking, reading, and writing processes with a heavy dosage of phonics at the developmental level. The following four areas, based on work by Pat Cunningham, were shared by Berglund (1996):

1. Guided Reading
2. Self-Selected Reading
3. Writing
4. Word Study (phonics, spelling, and vocabulary)

Figure 4.1 shows how the four areas will be integrated into my weekly classroom schedule.

Whole language can mean anything from teaching word meanings (while excluding phonics) to a philosophy of life as whole. No matter what aspect appeals to you, the principle of balance should be applied. From a reading teacher's point of view, the instruction of phonics must be balanced with the teaching of meaning. Whatever personal emotions one has about which aspect is most important, they must be tempered by what evidence indicates is best for the majority of students. Whole language, with its emphasis on learning whole words and their meanings, is of utmost importance very early in life. Phonics, on the other hand, is, as research shows, crucial during the developmental stages of reading. Consequently, a successful reading

Figure 4.1: Classroom Schedule Using Four Major Instructional Blocks

MONDAY	TUESDAY	WEDNESDAY	THURSDAY	FRIDAY
GUIDED READING (30–35 min.) Daily Comp. Strategies	partner read and discuss or literature circles/teacher guided activities	choral reading literature response books	write favorite part of story/share review any comp. strategies	teacher models reading as students follow along, discuss workbook work
SELF-SELECTED READING (30–35 min.) Daily teacher read aloud 10 min. student selects literature 20 min.	continue from Monday/cooperative activities	personal response and discussion	independent activities	additional teacher support activities for strategies, skills, and/or vocab. are provided through mini lessons, continue to read on own/partner
WRITING (30–35 min.) Daily mini lesson 10 min write time 15 min. share 10 min.	repeat	repeat	repeat	repeat
WORD STUDY (30–35 min.) Daily phonics, spelling, vocab.	practice with slates phonics/rules, word wall activities	co-op with group making sentences	pretest/correct using overhead practice misspelled words	test, practice and review any phonics/rules

teacher must have a balanced, well-integrated teaching approach that incorporates a strong phonics discipline with a motivating application of meaning emphasis. With these notions balanced, and one's emotions in check, the final step is to adopt the appropriate "potions" and put them into practice. It's time to plan your work and work for your plans.

Balanced Assessment for Balanced Instruction

Jocelyn Klotz

Recently, the whole language philosophy of teaching has come under intense scrutiny from parents, community members, and even some teachers who, before now, supported the philosophy wholeheartedly. Many people who are questioning the whole language philosophy are calling for "balanced instruction" in the teaching of reading. Balanced instruction means different things to different people, but in a broad sense it means a mix of traditional teaching methods and the more current methods, based on the latest research about how children learn. Ideally, balanced reading instruction would include an eclectic mix of methods so that all children would learn to read. In reality, balanced reading instruction is what many teachers have been doing for a long time: adjusting the methods of instruction to fit varying learning styles.

Along with the idea of balanced reading instruction comes balanced assessment. Balanced assessment, like balanced instruction, should involve many different approaches. Before planning for balanced instruction, teachers should decide on their desired outcomes and plan how they will assess those outcomes. They can then plan their instruction accordingly.

Why Balanced Assessment?

In a balanced reading program, we teach students to use many techniques, skills, and strategies. It only makes sense that we wouldn't use one assessment tool to assess all these different areas. "No single behavior, strategy, activity, or task can provide a comprehensive picture of student learning. Only a variety of measures, examined carefully over a period of time, can give an accurate and complete picture of a student's progress, strengths, and needs" (Routman, 1991). A balanced assessment "tool kit" is necessary to meet all the assessment needs in a classroom.

Assessment Tools

There are two basic types of assessment, formal and informal. Informal assessments are better suited to meet the day-to-day needs of a teacher who uses a balanced reading approach. There are several reasons for this statement. First, formal or standardized tests don't always match instructional methods. In a balanced reading program, children are not often taught to "fill in the bubble" during their daily work. While this activity may be used from time to time, asking students to show what they know using only this kind of test is not a complete measure of their knowledge or ability. Students are better served by assessment methods that match the instruction they have received.

Second, once-a-year standardized tests can be influenced by outside factors such as illness, personal problems, anxiety, hunger, and other factors that are beyond our control. By using informal assessments on a more regular basis, teachers get a more complete, well-rounded picture of their students.

Third, many of the standardized tests don't match the goals of balanced reading instruction. For example, in a balanced reading program, one of the goals may be for students to use different strategies when they come to an unknown word. This behavior is hard to assess through a multiple choice test. Many of the goals in a balanced reading program are not best assessed using standardized tests; therefore, informal assessments are more appropriate.

Teachers may choose from many different informal assessments. Obviously, every teacher can't use every assessment tool, and not every assessment tool will serve a useful purpose for every teacher. Teachers need to select tools that will measure whatever outcomes they desire their students to reach. Following are some commonly used informal assessments and reasons why they are useful.

Teacher Observation

When teachers carefully observe students during reading situations, they can note the strategies the students use (or don't use) to decode words and comprehend text. During observations, the teacher can interact with students and inquire about the ways they figured out the words.

Similarly, when teachers observe writing, they can gain insights into students' spelling strategies and phonic knowledge, handwriting difficulties, knowledge of story structure, use of resources, and a host of other behaviors. Again, interaction between the teacher and the student can provide better insight to the student's thought processes.

Observations should be recorded on a regular basis so that consistent behaviors and growth can be noted over time. The observations should be written as descriptions of the events and be relatively free of teacher judgment or interpretations (Rhodes & Nathenson-Mejia, 1992).

Teachers may choose from many different systems for recording their observations. For me, the easiest way to record observations is by using one inch by two inch "sticky notes" and a sheet of paper divided into a grid, with spaces the size of the notes. In each grid space, I write a student's name. When I write an observation for a student, I look for the appropriate grid space and stick the note to the space. I can tell at a glance who has not been observed yet because their grid spaces are still open. I try to fill the grid once each week. Some students may have several notes sticking to their space if there was a lot to observe that week. At the end of each week, I transfer the notes to each student's grid in their portfolio. The notes are then in chronological order for each student.

Teachers should look for evidence that their students are moving toward meeting the outcomes that have been identified as important goals for learning. If the observations lead the teacher to the conclusion that some students are having difficulty, an alternate form of instruction can be used with those students. This helps to promote balance in instructional methods.

Observation is probably the type of assessment I use most frequently in my classroom. As I observe several students each day, I gain insights into how they are progressing, especially when I refer back to the notes I have written previously. In the area of reading, my notes typically contain strategies the students are (or aren't) using, words that give them trouble, comments on their fluency as readers, and quotes from conversations I hear when students are sharing a book together. These notes are especially helpful when I need to give parents specific examples of their children's strengths and areas for improvement.

Portfolios

Portfolios, like observations, show growth over time. Portfolios can include work from all subject areas or from one specific area. They can also be organized to include only "best work" or papers that show evidence of growth and risk-taking. Work samples chosen for portfolios include written comments from the student and/or teacher. Portfolios may be maintained by the teacher, the student, or a combination of the two. In my classroom, the students and I decide together about the kinds of items that should be included in the portfolios. When students choose items to include, they attach a sheet to the work that tells why they selected it. As long as they have a specific reason that supports their choice, I allow them to include the item.

Like observations, portfolios are a good way to measure if students are reaching the outcomes that the teacher has chosen. Papers that show evidence of growth toward the outcomes (or lack of growth) can be saved. Tapes of oral reading can be kept in the portfolio, along with the running records of the reading, to show several different aspects of reading growth at one time (e.g., miscues, self-corrections, fluency, expression). Any evidence collected from the portfolios can be used to guide instruction and help the student move toward the stated outcomes.

While I have been teaching, I have learned several important things about portfolios. First, there is no single way to manage a portfolio system. Something that works well for another teacher may or may not work for you. Second, all the items you want to include in a portfolio don't have to physically be in the same spot. For example, in my classroom, students keep writing folders and journals in their desks, and I keep reading samples on audio tapes in a shoe box. Even though these things are not all stored in the same place, I can quickly gather them together to show evidence of the students' growth in these areas. I consider these items part of the students' portfolios. The idea that the items didn't have to be kept together made the process much easier.

Interest Inventories and Attitude Surveys

In a balanced reading program, one important aspect is for students to want to read. I want them to be lifelong readers. One way to see if students are moving toward that outcome is to interview them or administer an interest inventory or an attitude survey. There are many different inventories available in Johns and Lenski (1997). I prefer the McKenna and Kear (1990) *Elementary Reading Attitude Survey* (the Garfield survey) for my second graders. This survey can be administered to a whole class at one time.

If a love of reading is one of the outcomes that is decided upon, several inventories can be given over the course of the year to note changes in attitude. If student responses to the questions on the inventories are negative, teachers can implement strategies to promote a more positive attitude toward reading.

At the beginning of each year, I give my students a reading interest inventory. Because I teach second grade, I usually use one that doesn't involve long written answers. After I collect the completed inventories, I look for any that might show a negative attitude toward reading and question that child further in an informal interview. I don't want those children to feel they are wrong for telling me their honest feelings. I'll usually try to spend some extra time with them during quiet reading to get them interested in books. Another strategy I use is to pair those disinterested students with students who obviously enjoy reading, in the hope that a peer will be able to influence them.

Near the end of the year, I give another inventory with similar questions. Sometimes I use the same inventory, but usually I use one that involves more writing. After they fill out the second inventory, I like to have them compare the two and reflect on changes that may have occurred.

Reading Journals

Reading journals can provide teachers with a wealth of information about their students. After reading a story or portion of a story, students respond to their reading in their reading journals. My students use spiral notebooks as their reading journals. One spiral will usually last them the whole year. Other teachers prefer to make new journals as their units change throughout the year. Sometimes students are given a choice on what to write about, and sometimes the teacher will ask students to respond to a certain question. Both situations are beneficial as assessment tools. When students choose what to write about, teachers can see if they are always choosing the same kinds of questions to write about, if they know how to respond differently in different situations, and what information they can pull from a story on their own. If teacher-selected questions are used, the teacher can pick questions that relate to the outcomes that have been chosen.

The areas that can be assessed using a reading journal are limited only by the teacher's and students' imaginations. However, some of the more common areas of response include predictions, summaries, relating personal experiences, reaction to the story, choosing and defending a position using support from the reading, identifying story elements (e.g., character, theme, setting), and acquisition of new vocabulary (Routman, 1991). For example, during our Grandparent Unit, there are numerous questions I ask that involve relating personal experiences with grandparents to the stories we've read. For example, I might ask, "Have we had experiences with our grandparents that are similar to the experiences the story characters had with their grandparents?" We also compare grandparents from one story to another.

I have found reading journals to be extremely useful for assessing comprehension and improvements in the spelling of frequently used words. I also like to use them to have students do a written summary (retelling) of two books during the course of the year. I compare these two retellings to note improvements in this skill. When I ask my students to write in their reading journals, they are usually responding to specific questions that I have asked them to answer. However, I feel like I'm ready to move to the next level with my reading journals: letting the students write about what they want to write about.

Oral Retellings

After reading or listening to a story, students can orally retell the story. Retelling can give the teacher information about the student's overall comprehension of the story and knowledge of story sequence and structure. This assessment strategy promotes balanced instruction in several ways. First, students can read the stories independently, or they can listen to the stories as read-alouds. In this way, teachers can check comprehension of students at all reading levels. Second, teachers can use prompts when students are struggling with their retellings. Those students who have a good grasp of the stories won't need much prompting, and those who are struggling will need more help. The amount of prompting that is necessary can help determine which students need more instruction on the concepts that are being assessed.

At the beginning of the year, after a good deal of modeling, I have my students do a retelling of a story that they have been exposed to multiple times: as a read-aloud, partner reading, and independent reading. Later in the year, I try to find a book that most children haven't read and have them do a retelling after reading the story silently one time. Since retelling is a one-on-one activity, I usually use silent reading time to assess the children. On a simple checklist, I check off the story elements (character, setting, etc.) as I hear them mentioned. It does take a fair amount of time to get every student assessed, but the information that I get, and the time I get to spend with each student, is invaluable.

Checklists

Although checklists don't supply teachers with the depth of information that other assessments provide, they can be very useful in certain areas. Some areas where checklists can be particularly useful are: 1) having students read a list of sight words to see how many they can identify; 2) tracking the types of responses in a reading journal; and 3) having the students check specific areas of a written assignment before turning it in to the teacher or requesting a conference to edit. To match checklists to outcomes, teachers may prefer to design their own checklists instead of using those developed by other people.

Running Records

In a balanced reading program, one of the goals might be that students will use many different strategies for figuring out unknown words in their reading. One way to get an idea of the strategies a student is using is to take a running record of their reading. This is done by listening to a child read and simultaneously marking any miscues they make on a copy of the text. In this way, teachers can note any self-corrections for meaning, applications of phonics and context, or substitutions and omissions the students make while reading. This is a useful way to assess the students' use of reading strategies.

Running records can also be used to determine if a particular book is at a child's independent, instructional, or frustration level. This is done by calculating the percentage of miscues made during the reading.

I have limited experience with running records. I usually do several a year on the students who are struggling the most. However, one of my goals is to try to get a running record on each child several times a year. I don't know yet how many times will be manageable and worthwhile, but that will come with experience in using the technique.

Who Should Assess Students?

In traditional classrooms, most (if not all) of the assessment is done by the teacher. However, it makes sense to involve other people who have a stake in the students' education. In the publication by IRA (International Reading Association) and NCTE (National Council of Teachers of English) called *Standards for the Assessment of Reading and Writing* (1994), the importance of involving students, parents, teachers, and other community members in the evaluation process is highlighted. By involving others in the assessment process, teachers can present a more balanced picture of the students' progress. While different teachers will want to include different people in the assessment process, there are three stakeholders that all classrooms have in common: students, parents, and teachers.

Assessment by Teachers

The IRA and NCTE standards for assessment (1994) highlight the importance of teachers in the assessment process. Their seventh standard for assessment states that "the teacher is the most important agent of assessment" (p. 27). Teachers assess their students for many reasons. The main reasons are for reporting purposes, for planning instruction, and to evaluate the success of their teaching. While teachers are important in the process, students and parents also have important contributions to add to the assessment picture.

Assessment by Students

Students can and should be involved in assessing their own learning and setting personal goals. Students need to have a purpose for learning. They need to be aware of why they are doing what they are doing, or it has little meaning for them.

Students can assess their own learning in different ways, but two good examples of student self-assessment are portfolios and checklists. With portfolios, teachers and students can look for areas that show growth or that have been mastered. They can also look for areas that need improvement and use those areas to set new learning goals. In this way, students are aware of where they should be focusing their attention. By using a checklist, students can proceed through their work or note their progress in an organized manner. Checklists provide students with some independence to work toward their goals, and they help provide a balance because they allow learners to work at their own pace.

Student self-assessment is something that I am improving in my classroom. I have a checklist for written material that my students use before they bring me a paper to check or a story to edit (see Figure 4.2).

I have also used audiotapes of my students reading aloud to help struggling readers. Several times a year, all my students are taped while they read aloud. For students who are struggling readers, I may have them listen to their own reading so they can determine whether the miscues did or did not make sense. It is

Figure 4.2: Writing Proof Sheet

When you finish writing, check ALL of the following things:

1. Does every sentence start with a **CAPITAL LETTER?** Is the word "I" **CAPITALIZED** every time you used it?
2. Do you have a **PUNCTUATION MARK** at the end of every sentence? (. ? !)
3. Do proper names start with a **CAPITAL LETTER?**
4. Are the following words spelled correctly **ALL THE TIME?**
   and, but, the, they, when, what, was, of, that
5. Is there a **SPACE** between each word?
6. Did you use **NEAT HANDWRITING?**
7. Did you put in any **commas, quotation marks, and apostrophes** you know about?
   If you can answer "YES" to all of these questions, you can now ask for help or go on to something else.

important that they be able to evaluate their own reading for meaning and for use of multiple strategies.

Assessment by Parents

Often, parents will tell their child's teacher that they are or are not seeing certain learning behaviors (such as reading strategy use) at home, and the teacher has seen similar (or different) behaviors at school. This is just one reason to involve parents in the process of assessing their own children. There are many different ways to do this, but an easy way to get parent input is through a questionnaire or survey. Surveys can include questions that correspond to the outcomes that the teacher has chosen for students or to the learning goals that students have set for themselves.

Another way to involve parents in the assessment process is through periodic opportunities to view and respond to student portfolios. Portfolios can be sent home on a regular basis with a comment sheet, or parents can be invited to come to school to go through them with the teacher and the child. Issue a standing invitation to parents so they feel free to stop by and view their children's work at any time during the school year, not just at conference time. Several teachers in my building conduct "Portfolio Parties" instead of spring conferences. These parties involve students, parents, and treats. They can be organized to include the whole class at one time or several small groups of parents and children, depending on the size of the class. During the party, parents go over their own child's portfolio with the help of their child. As they go through the portfolios, parents fill in a questionnaire about their student's work. The "Portfolio Parties" are a true celebration of learning.

Three-Way Conferences

Three-way conferences involve the teacher, the student, and the parents sitting down together to celebrate improvements and set new goals for the student. Regie Routman (1996) put it best when she said, "Now it seems absolutely ludicrous to me ever to have an assessment conference to which the child is not invited. It is akin to our principal having a conference about us with a central office administrator and then telling us about it later" (p. 153). Why should students be excluded? After all, their learning is being discussed. Three-way conferences provide a balance between three different perspectives on what and how the child is learning. I plan to try my first three-way conferences this year.

Conclusion

Balanced instruction and balanced assessment go hand in hand. The methods of assessment we choose to use should help us determine if we are meeting our outcomes. By using a variety of methods to assess our students, we get a more balanced picture of their learning and a better idea of the outcomes that still need to be addressed. Balancing assessment isn't necessarily easy; however, the wealth of information it provides makes it well worth the extra effort.

The Challenge of Technology in Balanced Reading Instruction

Janene Bowden

Since the late 1970's, when I first taught, there have been many changes in education. With the advent of new technology, there will be even more profound changes in the future. In preparing myself to get back into the teaching field, I took a course titled "Balanced Reading Instruction," which stimulated my thinking about what balance will mean in the future. A working definition of balanced reading instruction might be: "To impart the knowledge of language necessary to understand the printed word without going to extremes."

The trends in education seem to change about every twenty years, sometimes from one extreme to another. Common sense would say that balanced reading instruction should encompass more than phonics and whole language. Other methods should be used to help individual learners. As we move into the 21st century, let's not abandon what history has taught us about these theories and methods. I believe the quest for the 21st century will be balancing technology with the human touch.

Challenges of the Future in Balanced Reading Instruction

Nicholas Negroponte (1996, p. 202) makes this point: "If a mid-nineteenth-century schoolteacher were carried by . . . [a] time machine into a present-day classroom, except for minor subject details, that teacher could pick up where his or her late-twentieth-century peer left off. There is little fundamental difference between the way we teach today and the way we did 150 years ago. The use of technology is almost at the same level. In fact, according to a recent survey by the U.S. Department of

Education, 84 percent of America's teachers consider only one type of information technology absolutely 'essential': a photocopier with an adequate paper supply."

It has been said that it takes 30 years for new technology to catch on. It has been 20 years since the development of the first personal computer. We need to spend the next few years retooling for technology. Already computers have made inroads into the schools. Many school rooms have a computer in them, but how are they being used?

I remember that in the late 1970's, our principal wanted the school district to buy a personal computer. The reaction was, "When we have some extra money in the budget for something worthless like a computer, we will let you know." Richard W. Riley (1996), Secretary of Education, in his third annual State of American Education address, outlined eight challenges for education. One of those challenges is helping students become technologically literate. We can no longer put off the integration of computers into our curriculum, classrooms, and lives. We need to be leading the charge, not bringing up the rear.

The Computerized Classroom

Technology is advancing so quickly that it is hard to speculate on what the next ten years will bring. There is already technology on the market that could change the way we teach if we only had the money to bring it to everyone in the classroom. In regards to balance in reading, students will not only need to decode, read, and comprehend words and language; they will also need to be proficient on the keyboard in order to write and send messages via electronic-mail. For those too young to type, there is software available today with word and speech recognition. There are also programs that will read handwritten words and put them into text. Scanners will scan any printed material through OCR (Optical Character Recognition), and put it on the computer screen. The computer will both increase the need for and enhance reading, writing, and language development.

Today there is wonderful software available for beginning readers. The *Living Books* series not only shows a story on screen but can also read the story in different languages and animate the story for interactive participation. There are interactive programs on phonics and children's writing workshops. With the proper software, computers can individualize a student's reading and language study. The software will not only present lessons but will also score and keep track of a student's progress and provide the next lesson, depending on student performance for a given concept, skill, or assignment. In the multimedia age we live in, these lessons can be entertaining to the student. The computer can be helpful in assessment and instruction, if necessary. It will no longer be just a word processor; it will become an integral part of a student's educational experience, whether we as teachers like it or not.

The merger of HDTV (High Definition Television) and computers will provide almost unlimited opportunity for access to global information through the Internet and World Wide Web. In research for this article, I found almost 1,000 references to "Reading Instruction," 3,000 to "Phonics," and 2,000 to "Whole Language" on the Internet. An educational service, Ask ERIC (Educational Resources Informational Center) has listings for 750,000 educational documents. According to Nicholas Negroponte (1996), in 1994, 20 million to 30 million people were using the Internet. He predicts that one billion people will be connected by the year 2000.

"Children will read and write on the Internet to communicate, not just to complete some abstract exercise. The Internet provides a new medium for reaching out to find knowledge and meaning" (Negroponte, 1996, p. 202). Through e-mail, your students can be pen pals with students from all over the world. Think of the possibilities for international experiences that are being brought into your classroom and students' lives. If there is a language barrier, there is software to translate.

Your classroom reference section won't be what you bring in from the library or the outdated set of encyclopedias you have on the shelf. It will include CD-ROMs with all kinds of research material. You can either access reference materials directly or by network within your school, using complete and up-to-date sets of encyclopedias, scientific research, and certain historical events on CD. These can be read out loud by the computer if the student has difficulty in reading. If you are studying a unit on Europe, go there via the Internet: web sites will have both pictures and video to give the flavor of the region you are studying. See the city, hear the sounds, and get a feel for the culture. It reminds me of the old newsreel series, "And You Were There." Now students will "be there."

Other technologies will bring the classroom closer to the living room. Homebound students will be able to be a part of the classroom via video conferencing. In the future, technology could eliminate the classroom altogether (though teachers may see this as a threat in the same way that technology sometimes threatens other types of labor intensive occupations). Students wouldn't have three-ring notebooks. Instead, they would have their own personal notebook computer or PDA (Personal Digital Assistant) to fit in their pockets. These PDAs are available today, but will become far more sophisticated in the future. Each student would use these to download assignments from the school's central computer and turn them in via Internet.

An example of the impact of computers and the Internet on reading can be found in "Project Gutenberg." Its goal is to encourage the creation, and unlimited distribution, of some 10,000 Etexts (Electronic Texts) by the year 2001. These electronic books range from classical literature to science fiction. They hope to eventually put the text of every English language book published on-line. At present, participation in the program is voluntary, and most of the books are in the public domain. You can find the Project Gutenberg Etexts listed in most Gopher systems on the Internet, as well as in all the major FTP archives.

In the future, books will take on a new look. They might be on CDs now, but in the very near future they will be on a DVD (Digital Versatile Disk). A CD today has 650 MB of storage space, which equals about 100 million words. The DVD will have a five to ten GB storage capacity, which would be greater than one billion words or two hours of video. New digital video players will be able to use DVDs instead of VHS tapes. As electronics are always getting smaller, CDs will be no exception. CDs will eventually be small enough to be loaded into the PDA. Of course, one of these small CDs will have volumes of electronic books. The books may be in color, interactive, and include video. They may also include phonics for the young readers, along with whole language instruction.

The teacher's role in the classroom in the 21st century may be very different from today. An up-to-date working knowledge of software will be a must. Computers may grade and restructure assignments individually for students for the next day, while teachers will serve as resources and monitor students' work. There will be fewer papers to grade by hand and less paper work all around. (Think of the environmental impact on trees alone.) If students are not on site with the teacher, the teacher can still hook up to a video conference to monitor trouble spots and ask questions. Within a few years, almost all computers sold will include low-cost cameras for video input. The library could be smaller, since the space requirements for electronic books are approximately 100,000 times less than the printed equivalent. In fact, the text (without pictures) of all the books in a typical school library will fit on a single DVD.

Balance in Technology

If balance is "to reach or achieve a state or position between extremes," we must find that balance in the future with technology. In the future, the teaching of reading with the help of computers will be fascinating and rewarding. Computers will become the teacher's aide and classroom helper every teacher wishes he or she had. They will be able to interact with the students, score tests, remediate, and to some extent, validate what we teach. It will give that one-on-one instruction that is not always possible with large class sizes. Technology will take us places; however, it might also get us into places we don't want to be. There will be those who will want to use the technology for 95 percent of classroom instruction, and there will be those who will resist using computers or technology in any way. We must find a balance between these extremes. We need to keep the human touch in the classroom.

Another need for balance in technology will be between the "haves" and the "have nots." Years ago, some districts were able to buy new textbooks, while some districts didn't even have textbooks. We need to address the extremes of public school funding for the purpose of purchasing not only the equipment of advanced technology, but the means by which to implement it in education. It is not enough to have the equipment; teachers need to be trained in the optimal use of this advanced technology of the future. All of the rewiring, Internet, CD-ROM books, etc., that are available will be of little educational use in the classrooms unless they are implemented effectively by the teachers.

Balance in a Perfect World vs. Reality

Wouldn't it be great to live in a perfect world, a world where the student-to-teacher ratio was small and where instruction would take into account individual differences in learning modalities? In a perfect world, we wouldn't have to worry about school budgets. There would be unlimited funding for school facilities, equipment, extracurricular activities, technology, libraries, and teacher-staff salaries.

Unfortunately, we are imperfect people and we live in an imperfect world. Student-to-teacher ratios are too high in many school districts. Student abilities range from one end of the spectrum to the other. There are a wide variety of learning modalities that teachers have to address in their classrooms. Inclusion is "in" right now (another subject that needs balance, in my opinion), so teachers take on the added responsibility of students with special needs in their classrooms.

In the real world, there are teachers who were only taught whole language in undergraduate training but not phonics and skill and drill techniques. Then there are the phonics and basal teachers who were not taught whole language. These teachers may be asked to integrate one or the other method into their classrooms, many times without much preparation or understanding of implementation. Along with integration and balance of programs and methods, I believe teachers need extensive inservice training and mentoring. Balance can turn out to be a juggling act.

In the perfect future world, all districts would have new facilities that would be wired for computer networks, Internet, and electronic devices. Everyone would be on-line with the World Wide Web and Internet. Everyone would be computer literate. Teachers would use the computers, PDAs, electronic books, and computer software to the advantage of students. Ideally, the teacher would not lose his or her place in the classroom. There will always be a need for human interaction and words of praise.

The reality of the future is that computers will not be in every home or classroom. Not every teacher will be happy about computers. Not all computers will be hooked up to the Internet. Not every school district will have quality interactive and supportive software. PDA devices and electronic books will not be available to every student. What this means to me is that those who have technology at home and those school districts which have the money and foresight to incorporate the new technology into their programs will have a definite advantage. The gap between the "haves" and "have nots" will get considerably wider.

Balancing reading instruction in the future may mean balancing: paper books vs. electronic books; what is teacher taught vs. what is taught by software; research on the Internet vs. the use of reference CD-ROMs; the use of game teaching software vs. pure skill and drill.

Balance may take on a whole new global meaning. In the future we might find out that phonics and whole language have meshed very well together. The writing skills of whole language have worked well with e-mail and communication on the Internet. Whole language has helped with integrating our subjects. Phonics has helped us learn to read and be proficient spellers.

Summary

The word "balance" may be the latest buzz word in education, but the concept is not new. Kathryn Carr (1995) suggests that experienced teachers are always using their professional judgment in adapting state curricula to individual student needs by balancing new and old methods. She goes on to say that we should place less emphasis on the program and more emphasis on teaching the student multiple ways to unlock meaning. I contend that balance shouldn't just take in the context of phonics and whole language, but all methods within our classrooms to meet the needs of our students. We need to learn to balance what legislatures mandate about methods and what our common sense tells us. I think it is very important to realize that balance doesn't always come overnight. We need the support of the local administration in order to adapt to change at our own pace while being given the proper instruction and mentoring.

I see the bigger picture for the 21st century as being "balance in application" between technology and the classroom teacher. The legislature will need to fund the retooling of schools to include technology. There will need to be a balance between the "haves" and the "have nots" with computer education. Classroom teachers will be balancing which software to use for reading with how much individual or class time to spend on the Internet. Do we achieve balance between the copier and the computer, or move toward less paper with technology? Will teachers have to balance this technology without the benefit of comprehensive instruction and mentoring? These are some of the issues about balance that will arise in the 21st century.

We are human beings and therefore have certain inherent needs. Computers cannot supply all of the encouragement, pats on the back, or glances that say, "you've got it" that teachers can. Computers alone cannot encourage the love of reading and writing. Computers do not show affection or love. Computers are not an end all—teachers will be the key to balance between technology and students in the 21st century. We need to remember the lessons of the past and use common sense with regard to the future.

Technology Bifocals*

Linda J. Conrad

Benjamin Franklin was a printer, communicator, politician, promoter of civic and cultural activities, founder of academic societies, and an inventor. Franklin invented bifocal glasses more than two hundred years ago. He realized the necessity to see two distinctly different areas with one set of eyeglasses: the near-sighted or immediate as well as the farsighted or distant. We might conclude that Benjamin Franklin was a visionary. We as educators must do the same; we must equip ourselves with technology bifocals to provide us and the public with a vision of a balanced educational system. We might even be so bold as to narrow this vision to a balanced reading program that encompasses all skills while being built firmly on a technology base.

Diagnosis

We work daily trying to furnish students with quality learning experiences. Monthly newsletters are sent, student abilities are further developed by building on individual students' strengths, and reading activities through novels are linked with the social studies curriculum. Reading is linked with art and music. Picture books are incorporated, and students engage in authentic writing. We use strategies to improve understanding and techniques to improve self-esteem. Drug education awareness programs exist, and classrooms are furnished with literature collections. Teachers assess learners, incorporate appropriate materials, and vary methods to meet learners' goals. Phonics, context, and a blending of basal with whole language techniques are

---

* In case you are wondering, Linda just started wearing bifocals.

all used. Instruction is large group, small group, or individual. Educators work toward cognitive and affective goals for their students. Yet with all this, are students adequately prepared for the 21st century? The prognosis appears (for many) that educators are wearing only their nearsighted glasses. What is happening to our farsighted vision? Are we capable of visualizing the impact our near vision has on determining the far ranging vision?

Denial and Trauma

Educators are responsible workers. Their major problem becomes the element of time. How can we get everything accomplished? In addition, when teachers invest a great deal of time in materials and methods, change is not easy. Mark Twain once said, "The only person who likes change is a baby with a wet diaper." Programs change. Superintendents change. Policies change. Does it make sense that anything should remain constant? Suppose the students we had five years ago did very well. Should something change that worked well then, and continues to work well? Why must we put on those bifocals and view a program from two distances?

I believe another deterrent for change is that some teachers stay in the same profession for many years. Educators are not forced to make the changes required of business employees. It is difficult for a teacher to relate to the frequent job changes made within the corporate world. I recently visited McCormick Place in Chicago, Illinois, for a computer show called Comdex. The exhibit required a guidebook of 188 pages just to provide a summary of different companies' computer software and hardware. One display gave examples of how to transfer employee names to different departments and different location sites. There were several concerns suggested by attendees about the frustration of constant personnel movement. Management wanted an easier method of moving employee names from one division of the company to another; sometimes the move was to another geographical location. Are we preparing our students with skills to survive in an environment like that one?

In addition, take a visual inspection of how schools look: much the same as they did twenty years ago. Where is technology found in a school? Is the office the only place where attendance can be done, and is it just in the media center that a single work station can be provided for an electronic encyclopedia? Would anyone want to go to an airport, a doctor's office, a bank or a grocery store that looked the same as it did twenty years ago? "The question is not *whether* to use computers, but rather how *best* to use them" (Lockard, Abrams, & Many, 1994, p. 3).

Prescription and the Correct Fit

Educators must keep learners in mind. A mission statement is needed along with a vision for the 21st century. Our students have to go out into the world with the skills of a lifelong learner. We have to work with topics rather than with individual subjects, with problem solving rather than with computation, with exploration and cooperation rather than with lecture and competition. Teachers must embody vision with the support of technology that is integrated into the curriculum. Teachers have to become less insulated and more global. Communities have to band together to support and upgrade schools. We must face the facts: life today is different from how it was ten years ago. Technology has to support the educational system. Education has to embody technology. This does not mean that we give up books, but suggests that we integrate technology into the existing curriculum.

The old adage "it takes a whole village to raise a child" is still true. It takes a community, a state, a school, a family, and a country all working together to educate a child. Educators must use whatever it takes to provide skills that will sustain students in their reading efforts. Students must read and read, and then read some more. They need to read the printed page as well as the electronic page. To that end, technology should be used as a tool for progress.

I agree with Lockard, Abrams, and Many (1994), who say, "As more and more written information has come into existence, problems of storage and retrieval have led to all manner of new devices—drawers . . . file folders . . . we are swimming in a sea of paper . . ." (p. 56). We need a method for the storage and transfer of knowledge. More than one-third of our students have computer systems in their home. The computer I purchased in November of 1995 is already slower than three of my students' computers. Six students e-mailed (electronic-mail sent from computer to computer via a telephone line) me at home with personal homework questions. The thought of being e-mailed two years ago appeared impossible. The truth is that some fairly teachable moments happened with the e-mail system, as well as the possibility of tapping into some special interest areas. A parent even called me to mention the increased interest her child seemed to have in the assignments as a result of being in constant contact. Perhaps the open communication was a catalyst.

Our class recently read a novel about World War II and discussed some picture books titled *Rose Blanche* (Innocenti, 1990) and *Star of Fear, Star of Hope* (Hoestlandt, 1993). I assigned a group of eight fifth graders to gather information about the Holocaust that would be presented to the class. This group used the electronic encyclopedia, researched information on the Internet, created a play, presented the skit, and designed a game for the class. By e-mail, they also contacted a friend who had visited a concentration camp. In addition, the group checked out of the school library nine more books on World War II and/or the Holocaust to encourage classmates to read other accounts of history. This group was full of energy and purpose. They worked cooperatively and were self-directed. The students also produced a notebook with the entire project, including game rules, using a computer word processor. I was disappointed we had not thought to call in the local newspaper for some coverage.

The use of databases enables reorganizing information, analyzing relationships, and comparing and contrasting groups. It is this analysis and regrouping of information that helps internalize knowledge and gain higher level thinking skills. Schools can buy existing databases with information about state populations, dates of statehood, square miles, physical features, water area, etc. Students can also create their own informational databases with research. They can keep a personal copy on a disk; a teacher can keep a copy for use now and later with another group. Resources can merge the student creations with the commercial products.

I have a personal database of all my music; some of the fields are themes, season, instrumental parts, number of copies, and dates used. I can bring a copy of the database to school for queries or information. After we had some alumni visit the classroom as guest speakers, I introduced databases with the simple problem: "How might a teacher have a quick, accurate, up-to-date information source on all previous students?" The students created the field titles of last name, first name, year in our class, student interests, and student visitations. Then, small groups entered all the information into the computer. Luckily, a young man now studying law at Northwestern University stopped by to visit during spring break. We went to our database and quickly found the information concerning his tenure at our elementary building. The students realized how the technological organization of information is a helpful tool; it can be practical and personal as well as scientific and very specific. We often wrote a hypothesis about a database and then did a query to provide the support. I had parents inform me that their child shared the hypothesis and outcome of such a project.

"Hypermedia" is a computer software process that functions nearly the same way that we believe the human mind operates. Hypermedia works with associations that are interrelated. A hot spot on the monitor screen can be activated so the reader can branch to a song, a diagram, or text. Hypermedia is a great resource in gathering information. Novels and short stories are already available on disk. The critical issue is that we get students reading. Reading takes practice and desire. No athlete qualified for the Olympics without doing the same task over and over; no reader loved reading without doing plenty of reading.

The New Vision

Progress must be our new vision. Information doubles every 18 months. Educators must keep program standards and support them with technology. We must provide a balanced reading program that includes phonics, a blend of skills in literature, language comprehension, real books, and quality reading. The *Standards for the English Language Arts* (IRA/NCTE, 1996, p. 7) state that ". . .students should develop competencies in the English language arts that will prepare them for the diverse literacy demands that will face them throughout their lives."

Authentic writing must take place as students see purpose and a sense of "realness" in what they communicate. This past year I had a student who was severely burned two years ago. The child was very scientific and creative. It was next to impossible to get him to put something on paper; perhaps his finger injury was part of the problem. Usually his one hundred word story sequel was only fifty words—and late. But once this child was encouraged to create his papers on the computer word processor, he blossomed. In fact, I frequently had to put a time limit rather than a word limit to his work! He had a desire to create and communicate when the computer was used.

Generally, I have found almost all my students to be more creative with the word processor—only a few students were more creative with paper and pencil. Furthermore, the students perceived the task of writing as more "official" and of better quality. We saved their work on a disk. Whenever I made suggestions for revisions, students were more willing to fix, change, add, and rewrite. Another interesting phenomenon was that cursive writing (even in fifth grade) was often viewed as laborious and time consuming. It appeared as though using the computer actually encouraged more student effort, commitment, and perseverance.

Telecommunication comes with a price tag. Computers are much smaller, faster, and more reasonable in cost than just a few years ago. Now, however, we require a modem to aid one computer to communicate with another. Since information is communicated over telephone wires, a dedicated phone line is necessary, due to constant telephone usage. We need a communication information service such as America On-Line, CompuServe, or Avenue to have access to the Internet. Once students have access to the Internet, they virtually have access to hundreds of databases, and the world of knowledge is within their reach. Students can obtain information such as the stock market prices, a total inventory of books in a particular library, medical research at the Mayo Clinic, or soil results of an agriculture project at the University of Illinois.

If a school has an LCD panel available, it can be wired to the computer so that the computer screen is projected onto a larger screen for group viewing and instruction. Our advanced math group used computer math games as a collaborative group activity or in small groups rather than individually. Computer assisted instruction (CAI) programs can simulate everything from a trip on the Oregon Trail to the dissection of a frog.

Conclusion

Educators must wear their bifocals for the vision to meet the challenge of immediate skill building, as well as the "retooling" of long range vision for future skills. Bifocals are needed for the survival of public education and student success. Educators must know what is expected next Monday as well as in the next decade; teachers must be the leaders. We must renew and refocus our mission.

Epilogue

The purpose of this book was not to present one view of balanced reading instruction; rather, the goal was to explore multiple perspectives and possibilities. Our aim was to provide an opportunity for teachers, teacher educators, and administrators to explore the benefits, outcomes, and logistics of a move toward balanced reading instruction. We hope that the teachers' visions and voices presented in this book help you to gain greater insight into how teachers can and do balance instruction in their literacy curricula and classrooms.

As we approach the 21st century, many questions are being raised about teacher education programs, how new teachers are inducted into the profession, how novice teachers are mentored, and what the need for professional development is (see Darling-Hammond, 1996; Shanker, 1996). The final article in this book brings those issues to life as Bryn Biesiadecki provides an insider's view of her transition from student to teacher. Bryn's experiences are not uncommon for many new teachers. She encountered inconsistencies between what she was taught in her undergraduate teacher education program and her student teaching experience. When she secured her first teaching position as a long-term substitute teacher, she realized that her education was only beginning. Bryn was fortunate enough to find a mentor in a Title I reading teacher in her school building, but all new teachers are not so lucky.

Many of the issues Bryn raises in her article pose real challenges to the field of education. As we look toward the next century, questions about teacher education, induction of new teachers, mentorship in the profession, and the role of professional development must be explored and addressed. As you read Bryn's article, we challenge you to consider how the teaching profession can help make the transition smoother and more productive as new educators move from the role of student to that of teacher. Such insights are vital if the teaching profession is to move forward to help prepare students for life in the 21st century.

From Student to Teacher

Bryn Biesiadecki

Things in the world of education are always changing. The pendulum seems to swing from one extreme to another—at least that is what I have been told. I am 22, and I will soon begin my second year of teaching elementary students.

Student Teaching

I received my degree in elementary education from a fairly small liberal arts college. The idea that the best way to learn was through modeling was definitely practiced in my education courses. Before student teaching, I observed for 120 hours at various grade levels, and in theory, this was great. But the different teachers had different philosophies. Therefore, one could do observational hours in two to three districts, student teach in another, and then get a permanent job in another. These experiences helped me find what I agreed with. Yet they were also overwhelming.

This is where my problem came into play. My first-grade student teaching was done in a district that had just moved to the whole language philosophy. There were to be no basals used, and very little in-service was given to teachers who had been teaching with a basal since they left college.

I did a lot of observing the first few weeks of student teaching. I watched the veteran teacher and tried to memorize the ins and outs of whole language as best I could. I had never seen this method in practice before, and had a very limited background in whole language. I practiced this method when it was "my turn" to teach and felt comfortable with it. I only knew about a certain way to teach whole language, this being the way my veteran

161

cooperating teacher practiced whole language. All I really knew was from hands-on experience, and I had little knowledge of the philosophy and theory behind it.

As I left college and my student teaching experience, I felt that whole language was the end all and definitely the way for me. Confidence was now a state of mind for me when thinking of the language arts; however, that would soon change.

My First Year Out

I was lucky enough to receive a half-year position my first year out of college. I received this position two days before school started, and I was ecstatic, as all first year teachers are. I would be teaching second grade in a district that was wonderful, yet a little behind the times. Basals were strictly used, along with grouping in some classrooms. There was a mixture of young teachers who used "new" techniques and teachers who had not even heard of the term Reading Recovery.

Being a first year teacher, without a job second semester, I went with the flow. I used a basal and tried to spice it up a bit with the new ideas I had gained from my student teaching experiences. I did not want to make any waves. I was also blessed with a Title I teacher who wanted a "push-in" program where she came into my room and taught with me. She had superb ideas. We got along and taught well together.

Every day, the Title I teacher came in my room for 35 minutes. During that time we co-taught the whole classroom. Students who were considered to be low readers intermixed with the middle to high readers. As a team, we mixed with and actually taught the second graders in my classroom. Even though I was a first year teacher, I feel that these children learned to their fullest potential. In fact, many children were dropped from the Title I program due to their progress over the course of the year. I received many wonderful ideas in reading from the Title I teacher.

My relationship with the Title I teacher was super. We could actually sit down weekly and discuss what we thought was best for all of the students in my class, especially the ones who qualified for Title I. We could both catch things that the other did not see. Until I went to my next school the following semester, I did not realize how invaluable the Title I teacher was.

This woman helped give me the confidence that I needed in order to grow as a teacher. She did this by giving me praise and encouragement. When she was in my room teaching with me, she helped me to recognize my strengths and weaknesses. She was full of great ideas and energy and was always striving to help the students as best she could. She also instilled this in me. She was a wonderful mentor. I only wish every first year teacher could have an experience like mine.

During my second semester as a long-term maternity leave substitute, I had the pleasure of teaching 22 third-graders. As in my first school, many teachers followed the basal manual. There were, however, more teachers who strayed from the basal path. I felt the pressure of finishing the basal in a short period of time without my Title I companion. In fact, after this semester, I felt I did not do as good a job as I did first semester. I felt this way not only because I was by myself, but because of what was going on around me. The other teachers in my grade were almost strictly using the basal. I felt that I could have done more if I had the freedom that I had somehow lost from the previous semester, or if I had been confident enough to take more risks.

My Future Class

I am proud to say that I will be teaching first grade next year for the whole year. I will have a freedom that I did not have last year. I will be able to take first graders through a whole year of learning experiences with me at the helm. I have taken two graduate classes to help broaden my reading horizons and build the reading background that I lacked.

Through these classes, I learned so many techniques and concepts that it has left my mind racing. I have tried out a few of these practices but not all. In fact, I'm glad that I have time to reflect and put together a program that I feel is useful. I know that no classroom is perfect, but I envision a classroom that will fit my students' needs and my needs as closely as possible. Most importantly, I visualize a classroom that will bring children to their fullest potential.

After reflecting long and hard about balanced instruction, I have come to know one thing. Every educator will have a different view as to what balanced instruction is. To me, that is what makes it balanced.

Some classrooms might use a little more phonics; others might use more whole language. There is no perfect way to teach reading. It depends on your individual classroom and what the needs of the children are. What might be balanced one year might not be the next year.

We need to remember our goals as we teach. What do we want our students to learn throughout the year? We need to come up with the best plan that we possibly can. We need to consider the technology and materials that are offered for use in today's society. We also need to look at different methods and the ways to evaluate those methods. Most importantly, we need to remember our learners and their essential needs.

References

Adams, M.J. (1990). *Beginning to read: Thinking and learning about print*. Boston, MA: MIT.

Allington, R.L. (1977). If they don't read much, how they ever gonna get good? *Journal of Reading*, 21, 57–61.

Anderson, R.C., Hiebert, E.H., Scott, J.A., & Wilkinson, I.A.G. (1985). *Becoming a nation of readers: The report of the commission on reading*. Washington, DC: U.S. Department of Education.

Avery, C. (1993). . . . *And with a light touch*. Portsmouth, NH: Heinemann.

Barr, R., Blachowicz, C.L.Z., & Wogman-Sadow, M. (1995). *Reading diagnosis for teachers* (3rd ed.). White Plains, NY: Longman.

Berglund, R.L. (1996, June). *Creating success-oriented literacy classrooms*. Paper presented at the Balanced Reading Instruction Conference, DeKalb, IL.

Bissex, G.L. (1980). *Gnys at wrk: A child learns to read and write*. Cambridge, MA: Harvard University Press.

Calkins, L.M. (1986). *The art of teaching writing*. Portsmouth, NH: Heinemann.

Cambourne, B. (1995). Toward an educationally relevant theory of literacy learning: Twenty years of inquiry. *The Reading Teacher*, 49, 182–190.

Cambourne, B. (1988). *The whole story: Natural learning and the acquisition of literacy in the classroom*. New York: Scholastic.

Campbell-Hill, B., Johnson, N.J., & Schlick-Noe, K.L. (1995). *Literature circles and response*. Norwood, MA: Christopher Gordon.

Carle, E. (1969). *The very hungry caterpillar*. New York: World.

Carr, K. (1995, Fall). What will be the next trend in reading education? *The Delta Kappa Gamma Bulletin*, 62, 49–53.

Chall, J.S. (1996). *Learning to read: The great debate* (3rd ed.). Fort Worth: Harcourt Brace.

Chomsky, C. (1971). Write now, read later. *Childhood Education*, 47, 296–299.

Church, S.M. (1994). Is whole language really warm and fuzzy? *The Reading Teacher*, 47, 362–370.

Clay, M.M. (1993a). *An observation survey of early literacy achievement*. Portsmouth, NH: Heinemann.

Clay, M.M. (1993b). *Reading recovery: A guide for teachers in training*. Portsmouth, NH: Heinemann.

Clay, M.M. (1979). *The early detection of reading difficulties: A diagnostic survey with recovery procedures*. Portsmouth, NH: Heinemann.

Cullinan, B.E. (1992). *Read to me: Raising kids who love to read*. New York: Scholastic.

Cunningham, P.M., & Allington, R.L. (1994). *Classrooms that work: They can all read and write*. New York: HarperCollins.

Cunningham, P.M., & Cunningham, J.W. (1992). Making words: Enhancing the invented spelling-decoding connection. *The Reading Teacher*, 46, 106–115.

Cunningham, P.M., & Hall, D.P. (1994a). *Making big words*. Parsippany, NJ: Good Apple.

Cunningham, P.M., & Hall, D.P. (1994b). *Making words*. Parsippany, NJ: Good Apple.

Darling-Hammond, L. (1996). What matters most: A competent teacher for every child. *Phi Delta Kappan, 78,* 193–200.

Depree, H., Bancroft, G., Anderson, C., Clay, M., & Giacobbe, M.E. (1990). *The story box teacher guide.* Bothell, WA: The Wright Group.

Diegmueller, K. (1996a, May/June). The best of both worlds. *Teacher Magazine, 7,* 20–24.

Diegmueller, K. (1996b, March 20). Best of both worlds. *Education Week,* pp. 32–35.

Estes, T.H. (1971). A scale to measure attitudes toward reading. *Journal of Reading, 15,* 135–138.

Fractor, J.S., Woodruff, M.C., Martinez, M.G., & Teale, W.H. (1993). Let's not miss opportunities to promote voluntary reading: Classroom libraries in the elementary school. *The Reading Teacher, 46,* 476–483.

Freppon, P.A., & Dahl, K.L. (1991). Learning about phonics in a whole language classroom. *Language Arts, 68,* 190–197.

Fresch, M.J. (1995). Self-selection of early literacy learners. *The Reading Teacher, 49,* 220–227.

Graves, D.H. (1994). *A fresh look at writing.* Portsmouth, NH: Heinemann.

Graves, D.H. (1983). *Writing: Teachers and children at work.* Exeter, NH: Heinemann.

Guided reading: The heart of a balanced literacy program. (1995). Crystal Lake, IL: Rigby.

Henk, W.A. (1993). New directions in reading assessment. *Reading and Writing Quarterly: Overcoming Learning Difficulties, 9,* 103–120.

Hoestlandt, J. (1993). *Star of fear, star of hope.* New York: Walker and Company.

Holdaway, D. (1979). *The foundations of literacy.* Portsmouth, NH: Heinemann.

Horner, B. (1996). "Storytelling." Lecture to Northern Illinois Reading Council. DeKalb, IL.

Innocenti, R. (1990). *Rose blanche.* New York: Stewart, Tabori & Chang.

International Reading Association and National Council of Teachers of English (1996). *Standards for the English language arts.* Newark, DE: Author.

International Reading Association and National Council of Teachers of English. (1994). *Standards for the assessment of reading and writing.* Newark, DE: Author.

Johns, J.L. (1994). *Basic reading inventory* (6th ed.). Dubuque, IA: Kendall/Hunt.

Johns, J.L., & Lenski, S.D. (1997). *Improving reading: A handbook of strategies* (2nd ed.). Dubuque, IA: Kendall/Hunt.

Johns, J.L., VanLeirsburg, P., & Davis, S.J. (1994). *Improving reading: A handbook of strategies.* Dubuque, IA: Kendall/Hunt.

Karlsen, B., & Gardner, E.F. (1984). *Stanford diagnostic reading test* (3rd ed.). San Antonio, TX: Psychological Corporation.

Kibby, M.W. (1995). *Practical steps for informing literacy instruction: A diagnostic decision-making model.* Newark, DE: International Reading Association.

Kroll, M., & Paziotopoulos, A. (1993). *Mark it!* Rolling Meadows, IL: Blue Ribbon Press.

Lionni, L. (1963). *Swimmy.* New York: Knopf.

Lockard, J., Abrams, P., & Many, W. (1994). *Microcomputers for twenty-first century educators.* New York: HarperCollins.

MacGinitie, W.H., & MacGinitie, R.K. (1989). *Gates-MacGinitie reading tests* (3rd ed.). Chicago: Riverside Publishing.

Manning, J. C. (1995). Ariston metron. *The Reading Teacher, 48,* 650–658.

Manzo, A.V., & Manzo, U.C. (1993). *Literacy disorders: Holistic diagnosis and remediation.* Fort Worth, TX: Holt.

McCracken, M., & McCracken, B. (1982). *Spelling through phonics*. Winnipeg: Manitoba: Peguis Publishers Limited.

McKenna, M.C., & Kear, D.J. (1990). Measuring attitude toward reading: A new tool for teachers. *The Reading Teacher*, 43, 626–639.

Morrow, L.M. (1993). *Literacy development in the early years*. Needham Heights, MA: Allyn and Bacon.

Morrow, L.M. (1985). *Promoting voluntary reading in school and home* (Fastback 225). Bloomington, IN: Phi Delta Kappa Educational Foundation.

Morrow, L.M., & Weinstein, C.S. (1982). Increasing children's use of literature through program and physical design changes. *The Elementary School Journal*, 83, 131–137.

Negroponte, N. (1996). *Being digital*. New York: Vintage Books.

Ogle, D.M. (1986). K-W-L: A teaching model that develops active reading of expository text. *The Reading Teacher*, 39, 564–570.

Paynter, D.E., & Marzano, R.J. (1992). *Literacy plus: Getting started in first and second grades*. Columbus, OH: Zaner-Bloser.

Paziotopoulos, A., & Kroll, M. (1992). *Literature circles*. Rolling Meadows, IL: Blue Ribbon Press.

Polacco, P. (1988). *The keeping quilt*. New York: Trumpet.

The Report of the California Reading Task Force (1995). *Every child a reader*. Sacramento: California Department of Education.

Reutzel, D.R., & Cooter, R.B. (1992). *Teaching children to read: From basals to books*. New York: Macmillan.

Rhodes, L.K., & Nathenson-Mejia, S. (1992). Anecdotal records: A powerful tool for ongoing literacy assessment. In *Reading assessment in practice: Book of readings* (pp. 138–145). Newark, DE: International Reading Association.

Richgels, D. J., Poremba, K. J., & McGee, L. M. (1996). Kindergartners talk about print: Phonemic awareness in meaningful contexts. *The Reading Teacher*, 49, 632–641.

Ridley, L. (1990). Enacting change in elementary school programs: Implementing a whole language perspective. *The Reading Teacher*, 43, 640–646.

Riley, R. (1996). *State of American Education Address*. U.S. Secretary of Education.

Routman, R. (1996). *Literacy at the crossroads: Crucial talk about reading, writing, and other teaching dilemmas*. Portsmouth, NH: Heinemann.

Routman, R. (1991). *Invitations: Changing as teachers and learners K-12*. Portsmouth, NH: Heinemann.

Schmitt, M.C. (1990). A questionnaire to measure children's awareness of strategic reading processes. *The Reading Teacher*, 34, 454–461.

Sendak, M. (1990). *Chicken soup with rice*. New York: HarperCollins.

Shanker, A. (1996). Quality assurance: What must be done to strengthen the teaching profession. *Phi Delta Kappan*, 78, 220–224.

Shaw, K., & Santa, C. (1993). *Pegasus teacher's implementation guide: Grade 1*. Dubuque, IA: Kendall/Hunt.

Spiegel, D.L. (1995). A comparison of traditional remedial programs and Reading Recovery: Guidelines for success for all programs. *The Reading Teacher*, 49, 86–96.

Stahl, S.A., & Pickle, J.M. (1996). A model for assessment and targeted instruction for children with reading problems. In L.R. Putnam (Ed.), *How to become a better reading teacher* (pp. 141–155). Englewood Cliffs, NJ: Merrill.

Strickland, D.S. (1995). Reinventing our literacy programs: Books, basics, balance. *The Reading Teacher*, 48, 294–302.

Sweet, A.P. (1994). Teaching and learning to read. *Education Digest*, 60, 52–57.

Swift, K. (1993). Try reading workshop in your classroom. *The Reading Teacher, 46,* 366–371.

Tompkins, G. (1994). *Teaching writing: Balancing process and product.* New York: Macmillan.

Touchstone Applied Science Associates. (1995). *Degrees of reading power.* Brewster, NY: Author.

Trachtenburg, P. (1990). Using children's literature to enhance phonics instruction. *The Reading Teacher, 43,* 648–654.

Trelease, J. (1989). *The new read-aloud handbook.* New York: Penguin.

U.S. Postal Service. (1991). *Wee deliver: In-school postal service.* Washington, DC: Author (Write U.S. Postal Service, Literacy Programs, Marketing and Product Publicity, 475 L'Enfant Plaza, Room 5300, Washington, DC 20260-3100).

Wilde, S. (1992). *You kan red this.* Portsmouth, NH: Heinemann.

Wiseman, B. (1989). The surprise letters. In *Sandcastles.* Chicago: Harcourt Brace Jovanovich.

Wray, D. (1989). Reading: The new debate. *Reading, 23,* 2–8.

Index

A

Ability groups, 73
Advanced Reading Strategies (ARS), 107–10
Alan Review, The, 125
Anthologies, literature, 18, 84, 89, 92
"Ask" strategy, 26–28
Assessment
 informal, 135
 by observation, 136
 by parents, 143
 standardized, 54
 by students, 141–42
Assessment tools, for balanced instruction, 135–42
 attitude surveys, 137–38
 checklists, 140
 interest inventories, 137–38
 oral retellings, 139–40
 reading journals, 138–39
 running records, 140–41
 teacher observation, 135–37
Attitude surveys, 137–38
Author study, 96–100

B

Balanced approach, 5
 major areas characterizing, 26–29
 reasons influencing need for, 24–26
 search for, 3–6
Balanced assessment, 134–44
Balanced day, described, 59–61
Balanced language curriculum, 14–23

Balanced literacy
 degree of emphasis, 38–39
 personal struggles, 39–40
 in primary classroom, 32
Balanced reading, case studies, 54–59, 126–33
 assessment, 56–57
 home involvement, 57–59
 reading, 54–55
 skills, 56
 writing, 55
Balanced reading instruction, 134–44
 in first-grade classroom, 41–47, 72, 88–105
 overview, 7–23
 second grade, 41–47
 and technology, 145–51
 third-grade view, 24–30
 transferring from basal program, 8–13
Balanced reading program, first- and second-grade classroom, 41–47
 developmental component, 41–43
 functional component, 43–44
 multi-year grouping, 46–47
 recreational component, 44
 Title I children in, 44–45
 and writing, 45–46
Basal reading, 8–10, 18, 43, 52, 72, 83
Basal reading program, skills-based, 62–70
 library for, 66
 read-aloud times, 67